## OLSAT® Preparation Guide II (Level A)
## Questions For Children

Written and published by: Bright Kids NYC

The Otis-Lennon School Ability Test (OLSAT®) is a registered trademark of NCS Pearson Inc. Pearson Inc. neither endorses nor supports the content of the OLSAT® Practice Test.

Corporate Headquarters:
Bright Kids NYC Inc.
225 Broadway, Suite 1504
New York, NY 10007

Phone: 917-539-4575
Email: info@brightkidsnyc.com
www.brightkidsnyc.com

## Table of Contents

**OLSAT® Preparation Guide II (Level A)**

## About Bright Kids NYC

Bright Kids NYC was founded in New York City to provide language arts and math enrichment for young children and to educate parents about standardized tests through workshops and consultations, as well as to prepare young children for such tests though assessments, tutoring, and publications. Our philosophy is that regardless of age, test taking is a skill that can be acquired and mastered through practice.

At Bright Kids NYC, we strive to provide the best learning materials. Our publications are truly unique. First, all of our books have been created by qualified psychologists, learning specialists, and teachers. Second, our books have been tested by hundreds of children in our tutoring practice. Since children can make associations that many adults cannot, testing of materials by children is critical to creating successful test preparation guides. Finally, our learning specialists and teaching staff have provided practical strategies and tips so parents can best help their child prepare to compete successfully on standardized tests.

Feel free to contact us should you have any questions.

Corporate Headquarters:
Bright Kids NYC Inc.
225 Broadway, Suite 1504
New York, New York 10007

Phone: 917-539-4575
Email: info@brightkidsnyc.com
www.brightkidsnyc.com

**OLSAT®Preparation Guide II (Level A)** Bright Kids NYC Inc ©

# Introduction

Every year, thousands of young children in the United States take standardized tests required by their school systems for entry into gifted programs, classroom placements, and school readiness evaluations.

The objective of the *Bright Kids OLSAT® Preparation Guide,* is to familiarize children with the content and the format of the OLSAT®. Children, no matter how bright they are, do not always perform well when they are not accustomed to the format and the structure of a test. Children can misunderstand the directions, fail to look at all the answer choices, and may not always listen carefully to the questions. Thus, without adequate preparation and familiarization, children may not always perform to the best of their ability on standardized tests such as the OLSAT®. The practice material in the *Guide* exposes children to the OLSAT® format, questions, and language to reduce anxiety and confusion prior to formal testing. There are 220 practice questions in this *Guide.*

The *Bright Kids OLSAT® Preparation Guide* can be used together with our OLSAT® Level A Practice Tests. Our OLSAT® Practice Tests can be used before working through this *Guide* as a diagnostic or after to assess test readiness. We also have supplemental books available that teach children the underlying core concepts such as The Bright Kids Core Concepts Workbook as well as the Figural Analogies and Picture Analogies books. Please visit our website for supplemental publications.

Children will be taking many standardized tests throughout their school years. Teaching your child critical-thinking skills along with test-taking strategies at a young age will benefit your child for many years to come. Our philosophy is that regardless of age, test taking is a skill than can be acquired and mastered through practice.

# Section One

# Following Directions

**OLSAT® Preparation Guide II (Level A)** Bright Kids NYC Inc ©

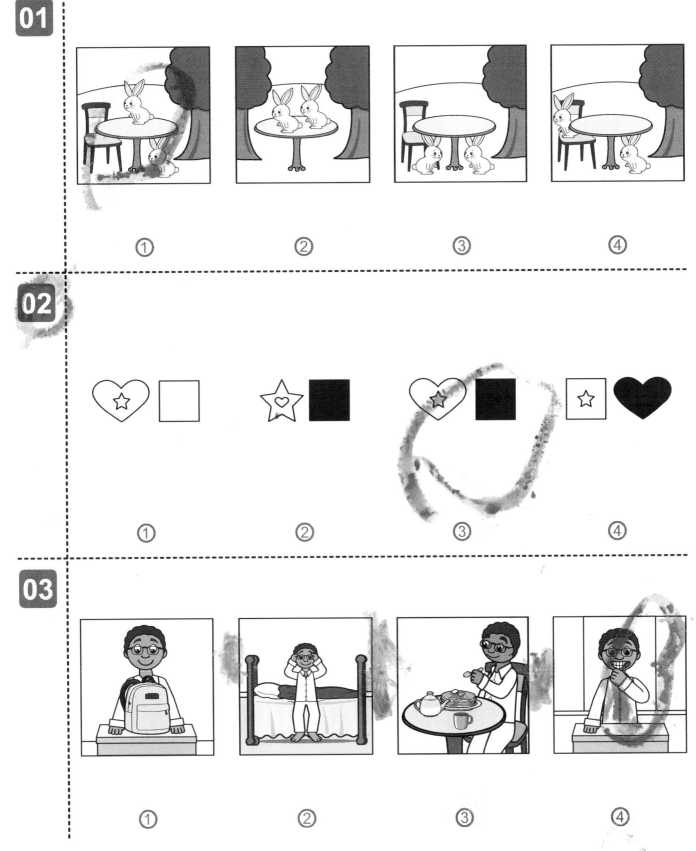

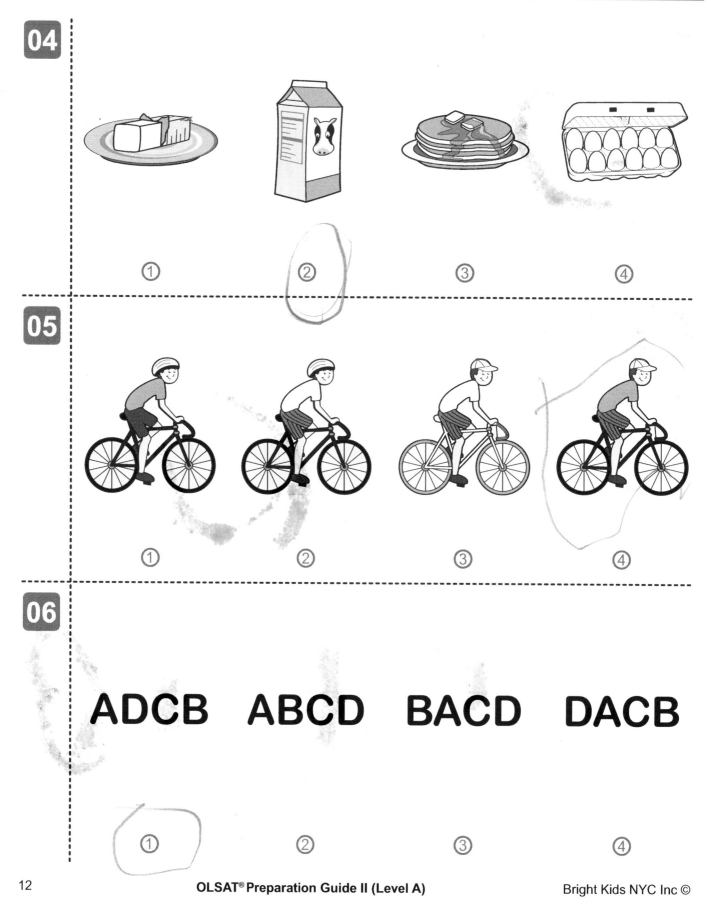

**04**

① ② ③ ④

**05**

① ② ③ ④

**06**

# ADCB   ABCD   BACD   DACB

① ② ③ ④

**OLSAT® Preparation Guide II (Level A)** Bright Kids NYC Inc ©

**07**

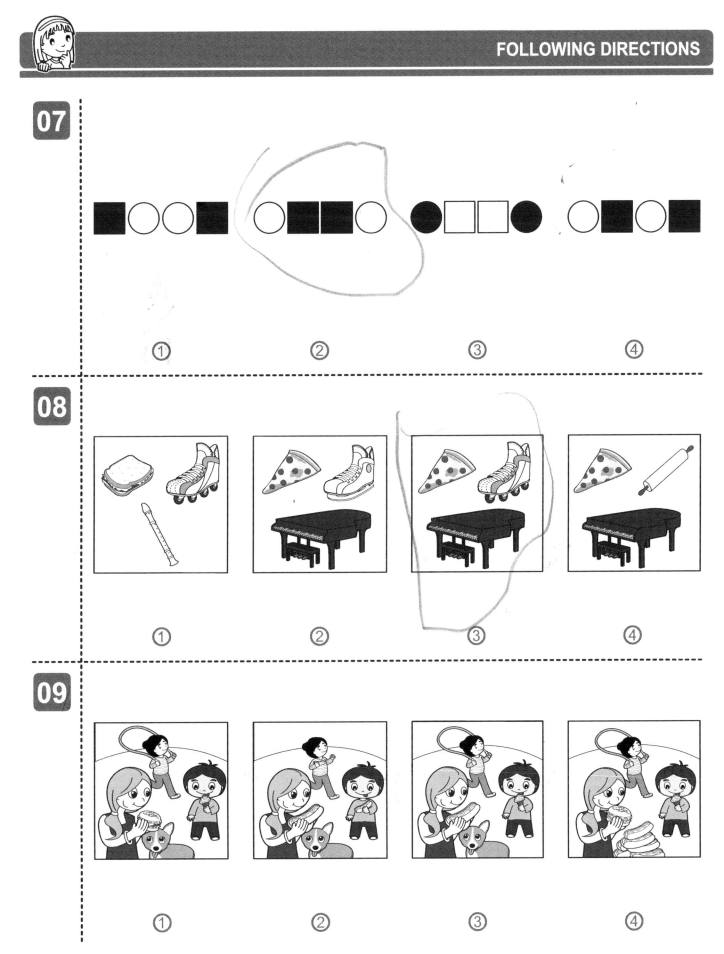

①      ②      ③      ④

**08**

①      ②      ③      ④

**09**

①      ②      ③      ④

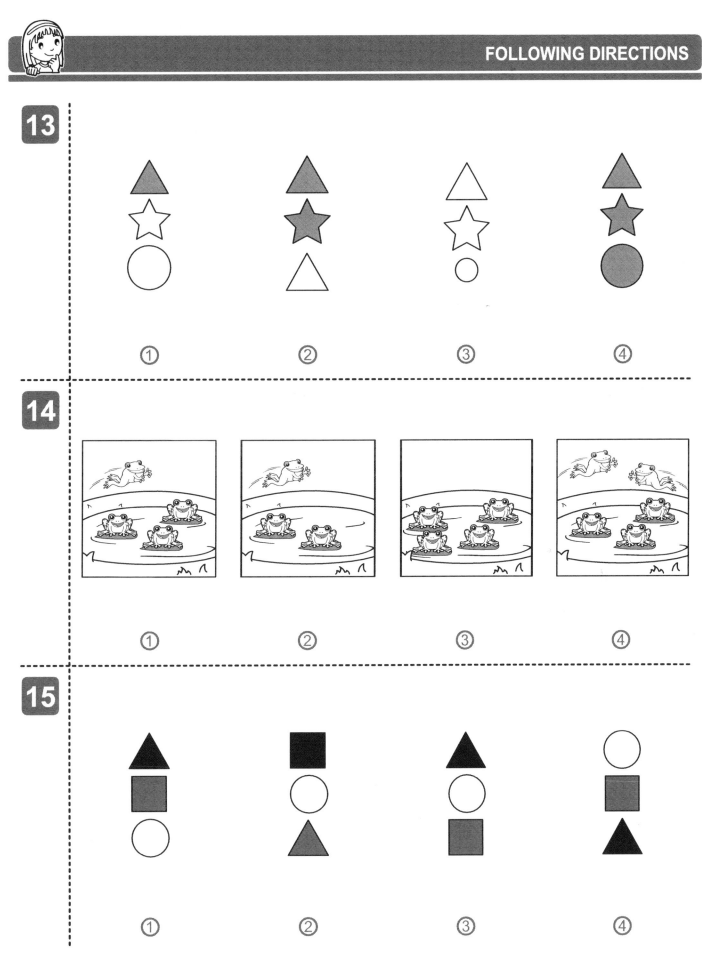

**16**

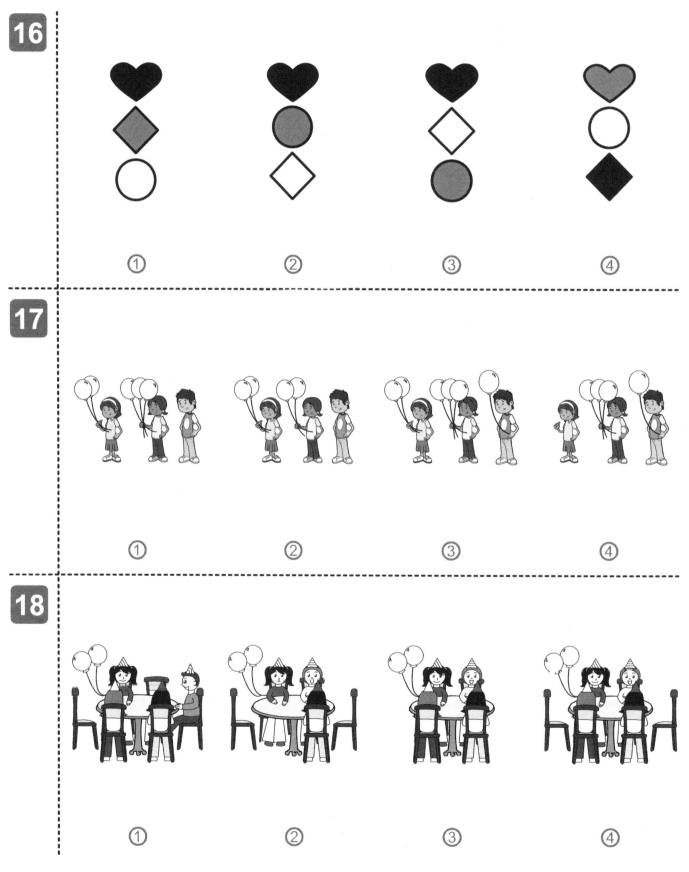

① ② ③ ④

**17**

① ② ③ ④

**18**

① ② ③ ④

**OLSAT® Preparation Guide II (Level A)**

Bright Kids NYC Inc ©

**19**

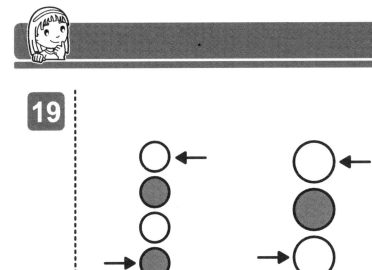

① ② ③ ④

**20**

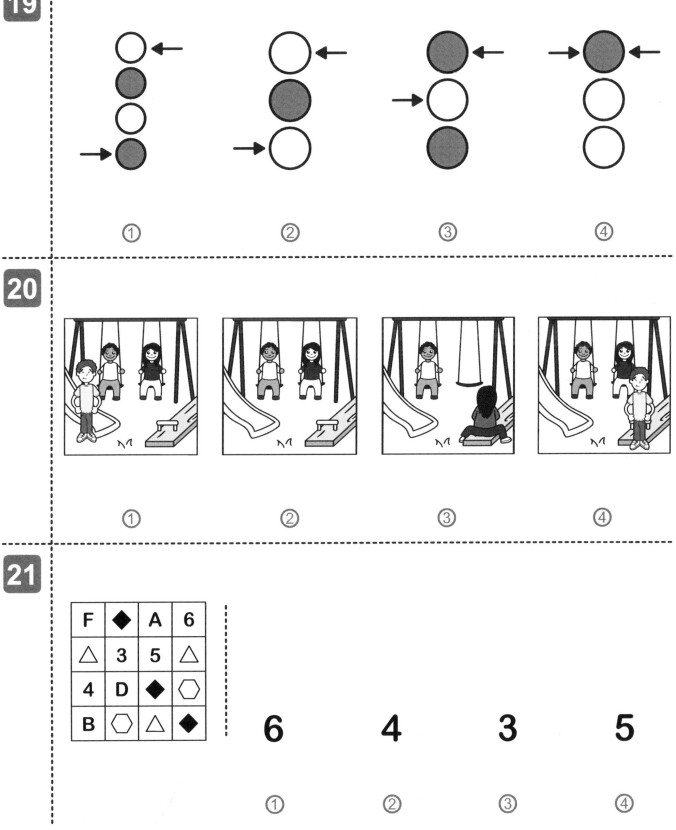

① ② ③ ④

**21**

| F | ◆ | A | 6 |
|---|---|---|---|
| △ | 3 | 5 | △ |
| 4 | D | ◆ | ⬡ |
| B | ⬡ | △ | ◆ |

**6**      **4**      **3**      **5**

① ② ③ ④

**22**

| 7 | R | ★ | K |
|---|---|---|---|
| ⬠ | ○ | G | ★ |
| H | ★ | 8 | ▽ |
| ○ | ⬠ | ▽ | ⬠ |

R     H     K     G

①     ②     ③     ④

**23**

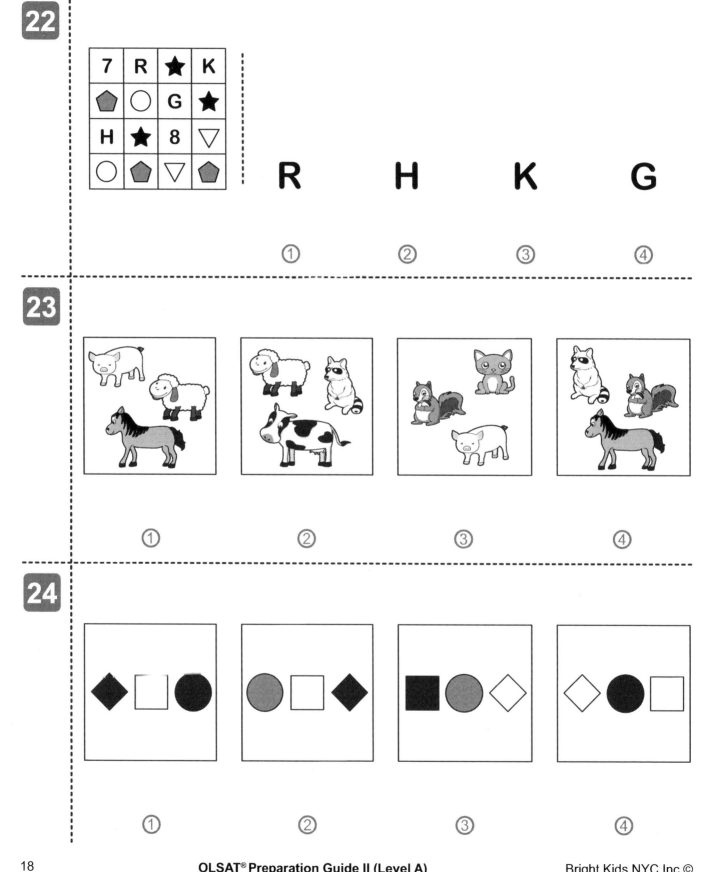

①     ②     ③     ④

**24**

①     ②     ③     ④

**25**

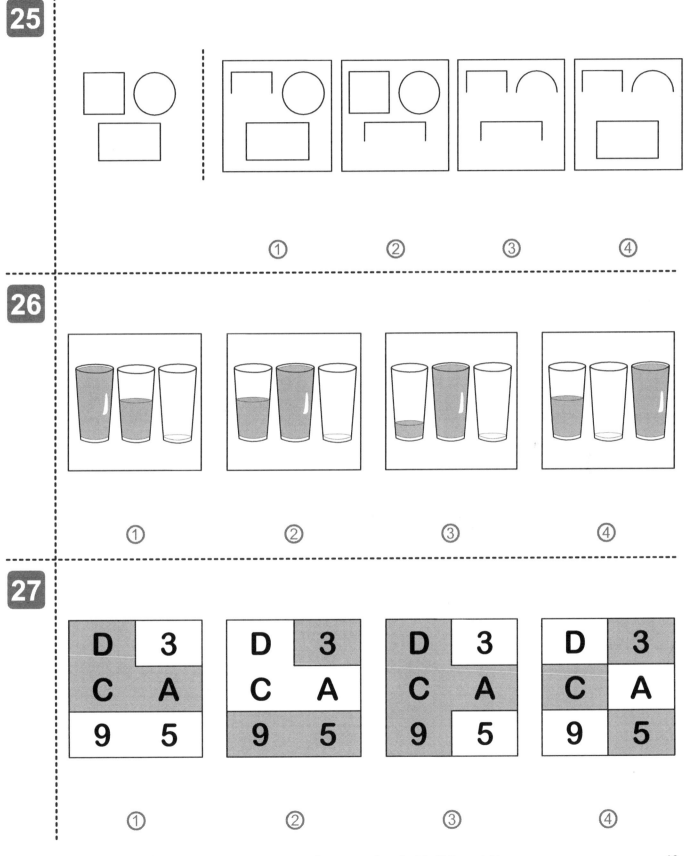

**28**

① ② ③ ④

**29**

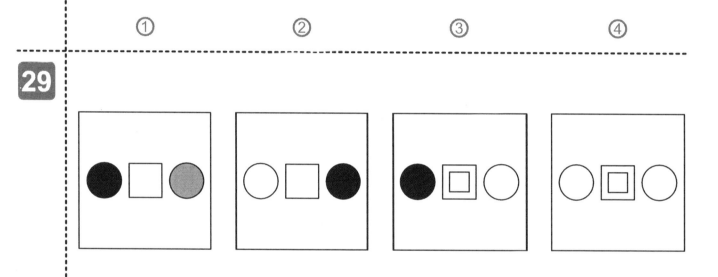

① ② ③ ④

**30**

① ② ③ ④

**31**

**32**

**33**

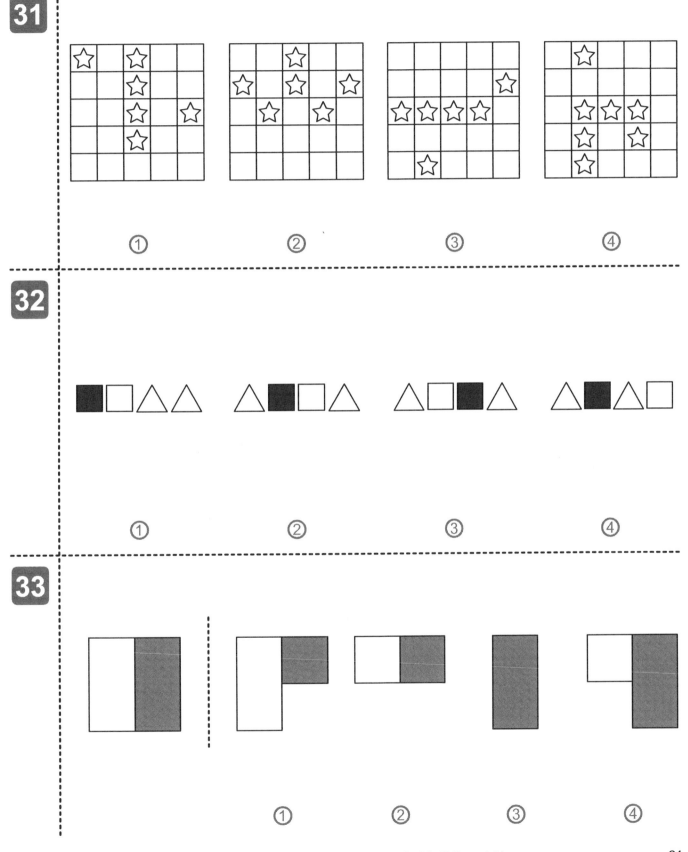

**34**

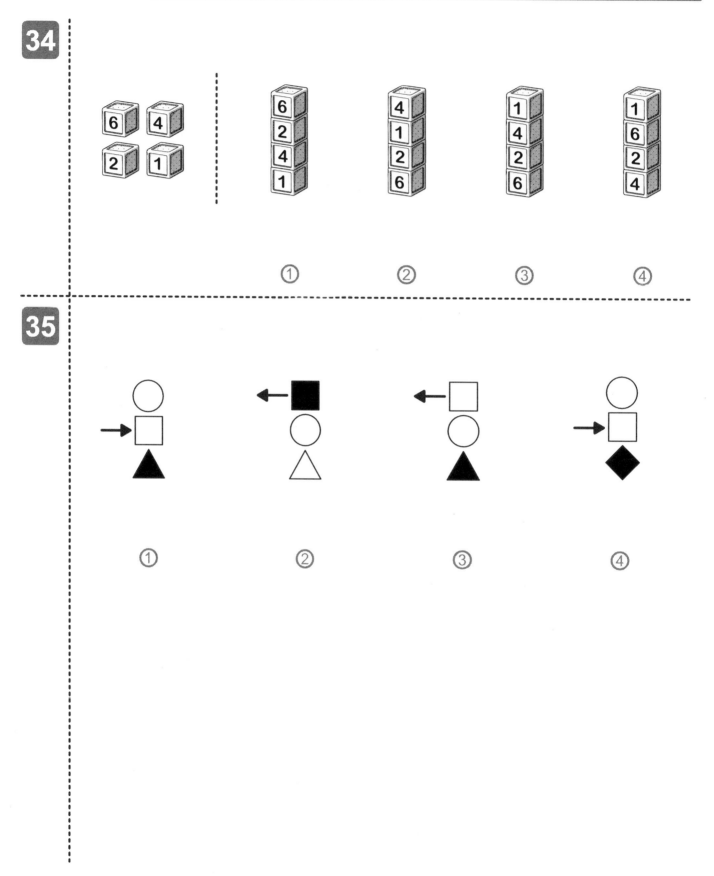

①  ②  ③  ④

**35**

①  ②  ③  ④

# Section Two

# Aural Reasoning

**01**

①　②　③　④

**02**

①　②　③　④

**03**

①　②　③　④

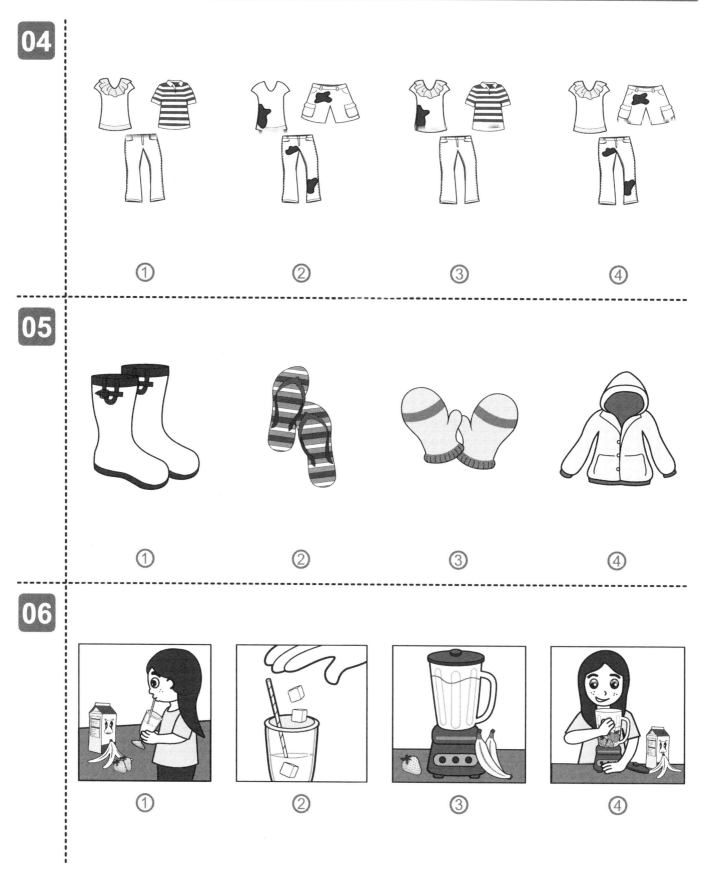

07

① ② ③ ④

08

① ② ③ ④

09

| JOHN | john | JOHN | John |
| 1 | 1 | 1 | 1 |

① ② ③ ④

**10**

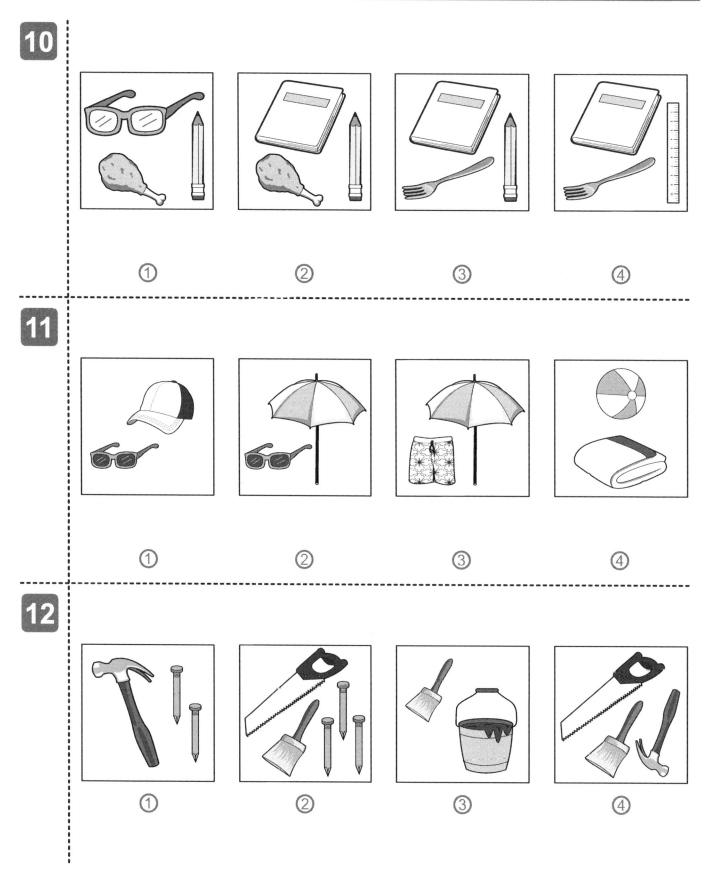

① ② ③ ④

**11**

① ② ③ ④

**12**

① ② ③ ④

**OLSAT® Preparation Guide II (Level A)**

13

① ② ③ ④

14

① ② ③ ④

15

① ② ③ ④

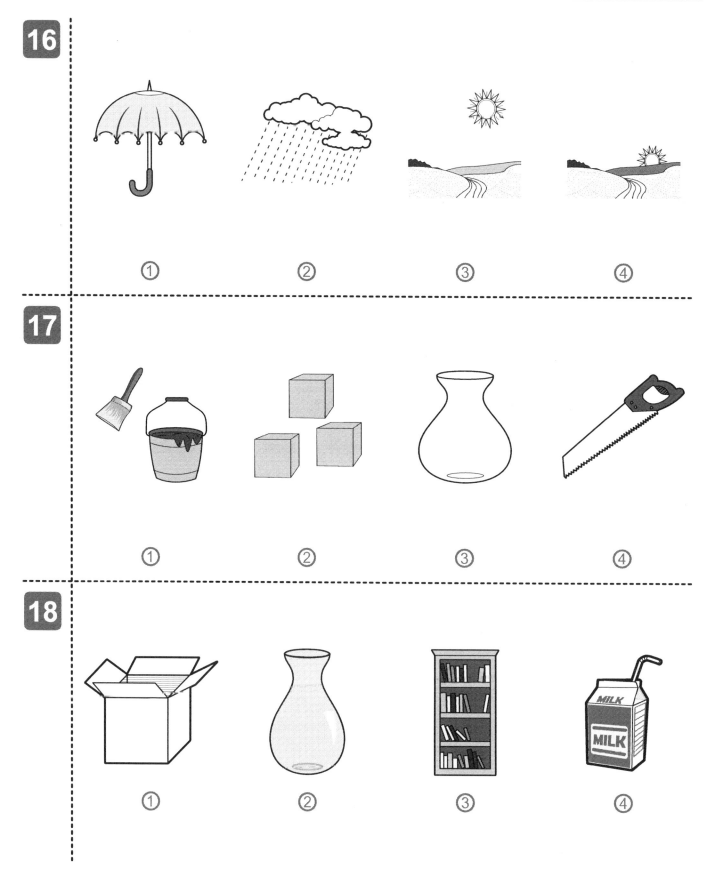

**16**

① ② ③ ④

**17**

① ② ③ ④

**18**

① ② ③ ④

**19**

① ② ③ ④

**20**

① ② ③ ④

**21**

① ② ③ ④

**22**

①　　　　②　　　　③　　　　④

**23**

①　　　　②　　　　③　　　　④

**24**

①　　　　②　　　　③　　　　④

**25**

① ② ③ ④

**26**

① ② ③ ④

**27**

① ② ③ ④

**28**

① ② ③ ④

**29**

① ② ③ ④

**30**

① ② ③ ④

**OLSAT® Preparation Guide II (Level A)**

# Section Three

# Arithmetic Reasoning

**OLSAT®Preparation Guide II (Level A)**

Bright Kids NYC Inc ©

**04**

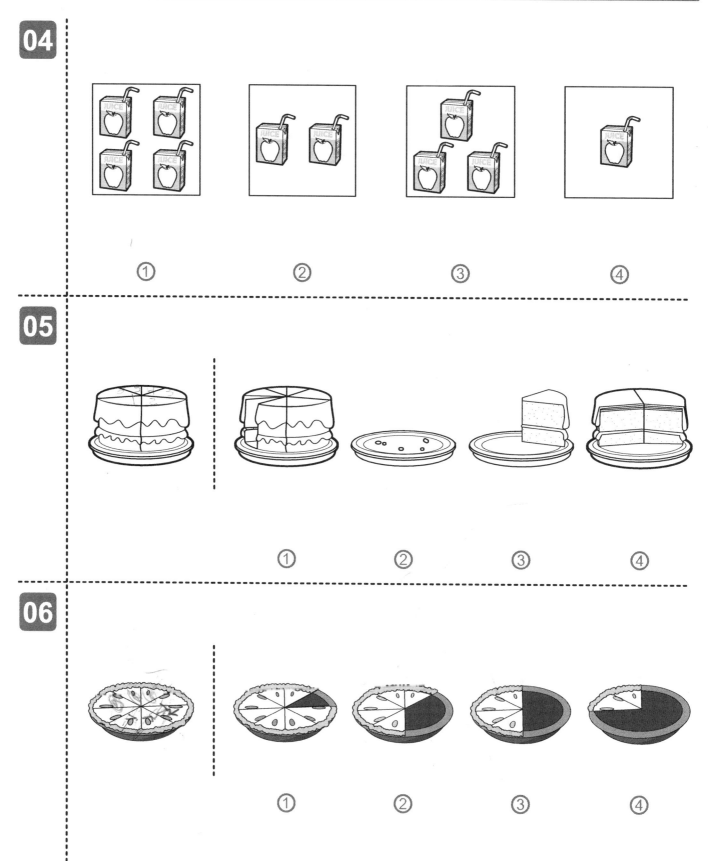

**OLSAT® Preparation Guide II (Level A)**

Bright Kids NYC Inc ©

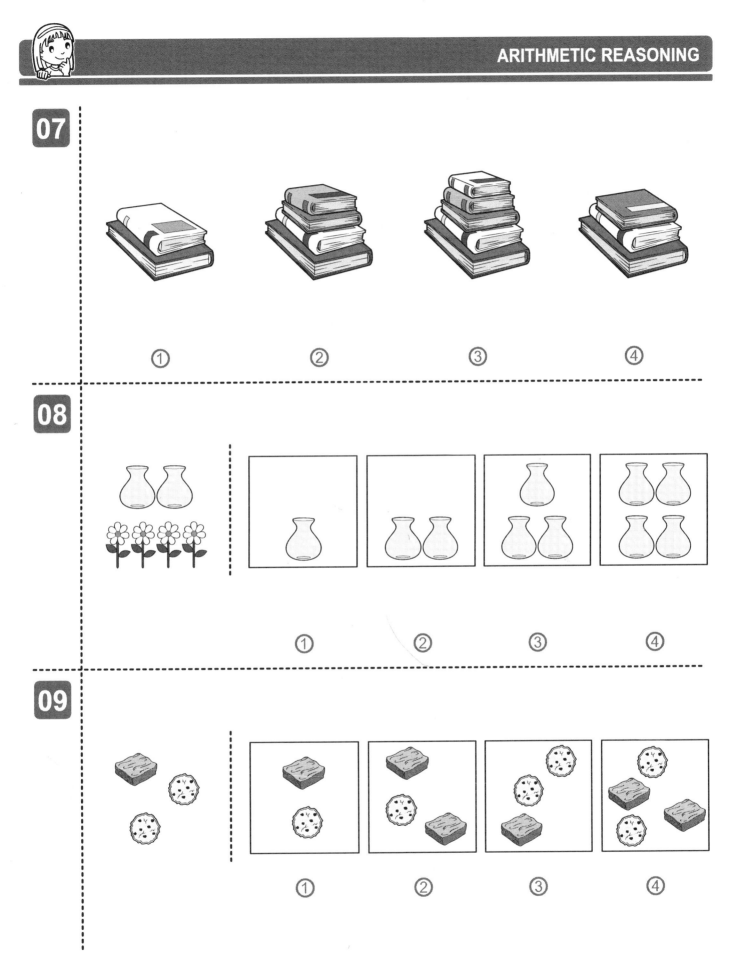

**10**

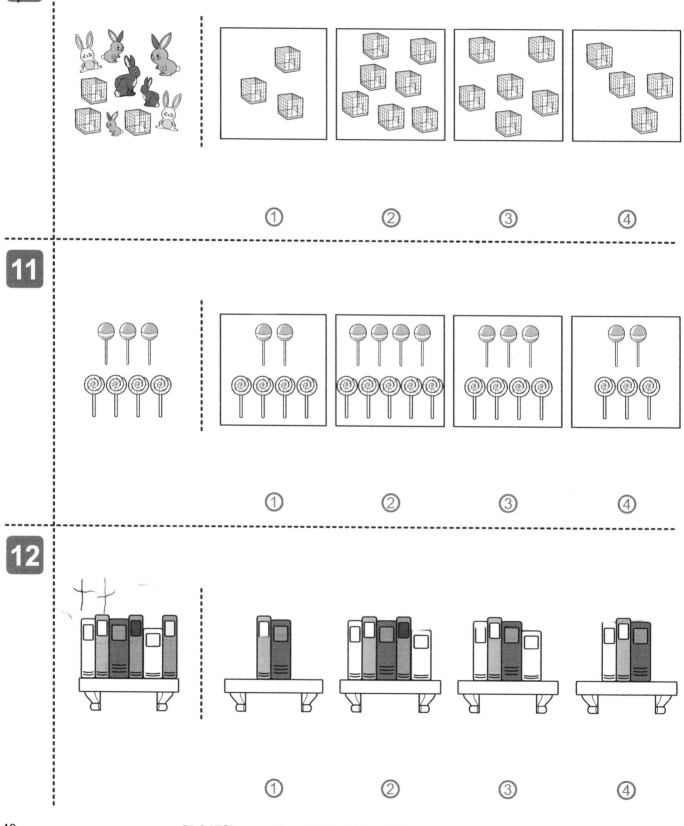

①      ②      ③      ④

**11**

①      ②      ③      ④

**12**

①      ②      ③      ④

**13**

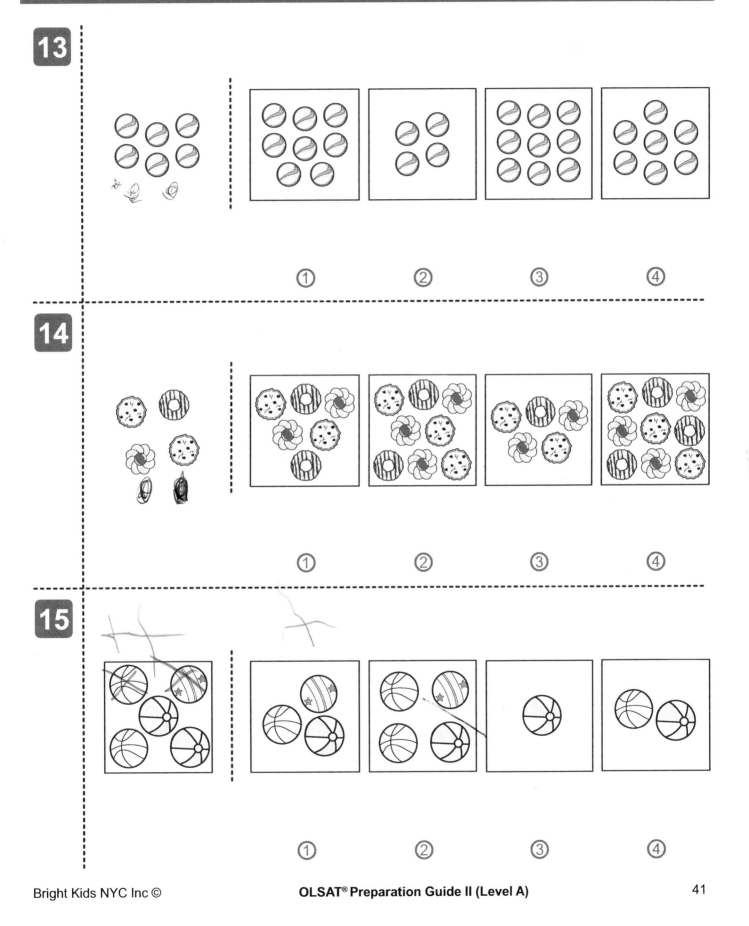

①     ②     ③     ④

**14**

①     ②     ③     ④

**15**

①     ②     ③     ④

**16**

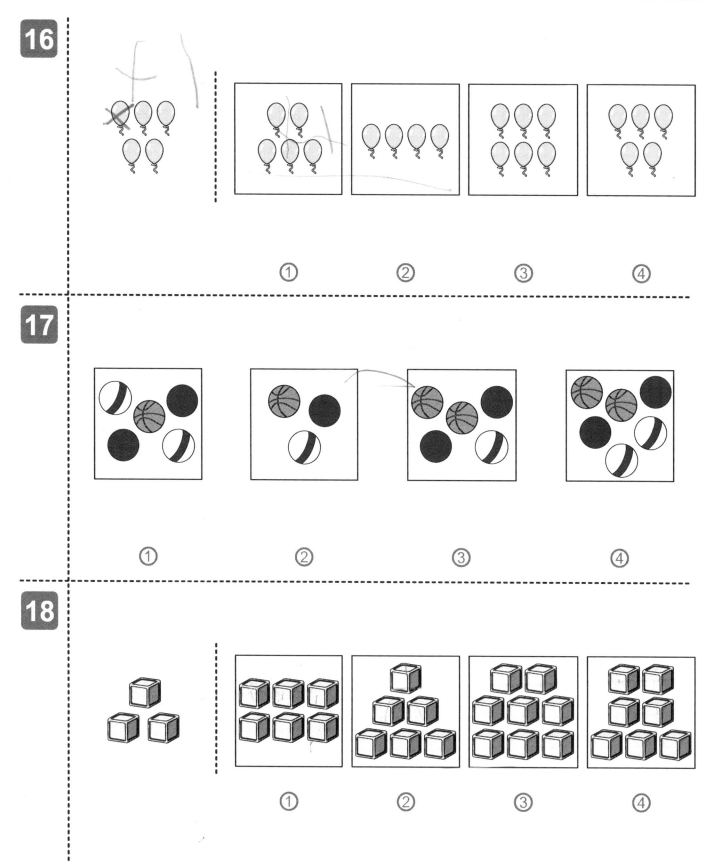

① ② ③ ④

**17**

① ② ③ ④

**18**

① ② ③ ④

**19**

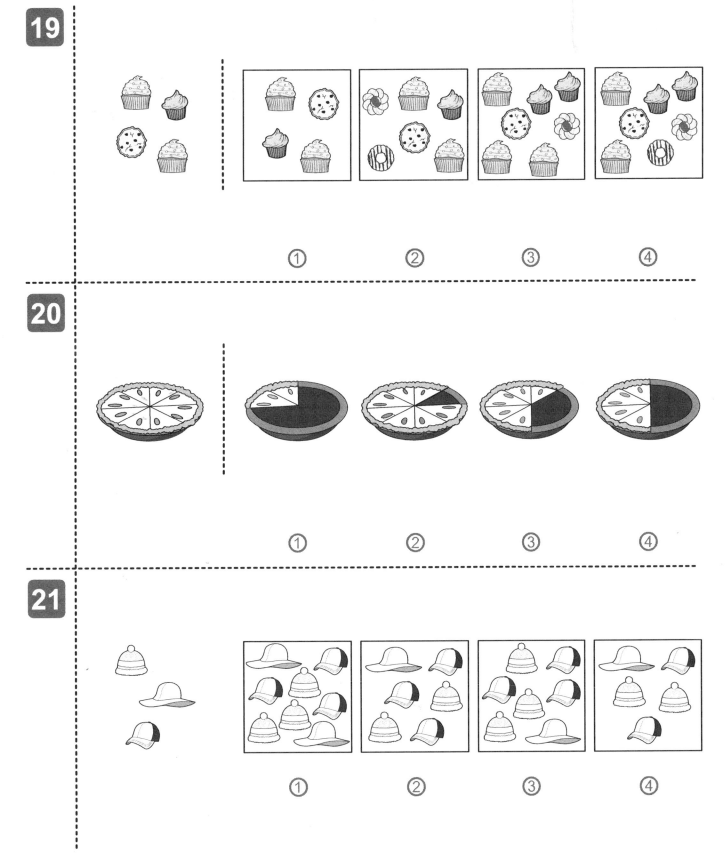

**22**

①  ②  ③  ④

**23**

①  ②  ③  ④

**24**

①  ②  ③  ④

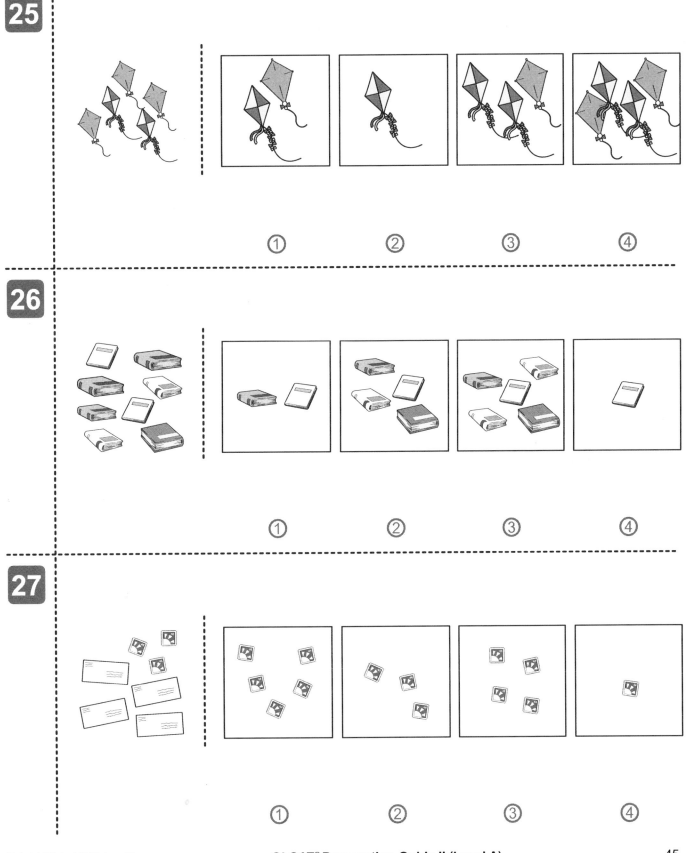

**28**

**29**

**30**

① ② ③ ④

**OLSAT® Preparation Guide II (Level A)**

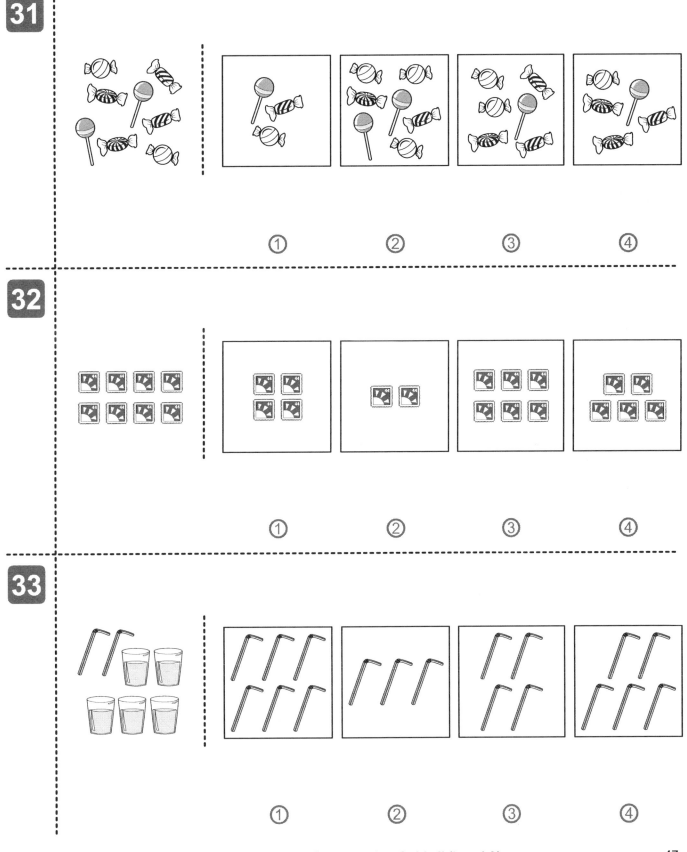

**31**

① ② ③ ④

**32**

① ② ③ ④

**33**

① ② ③ ④

**34**

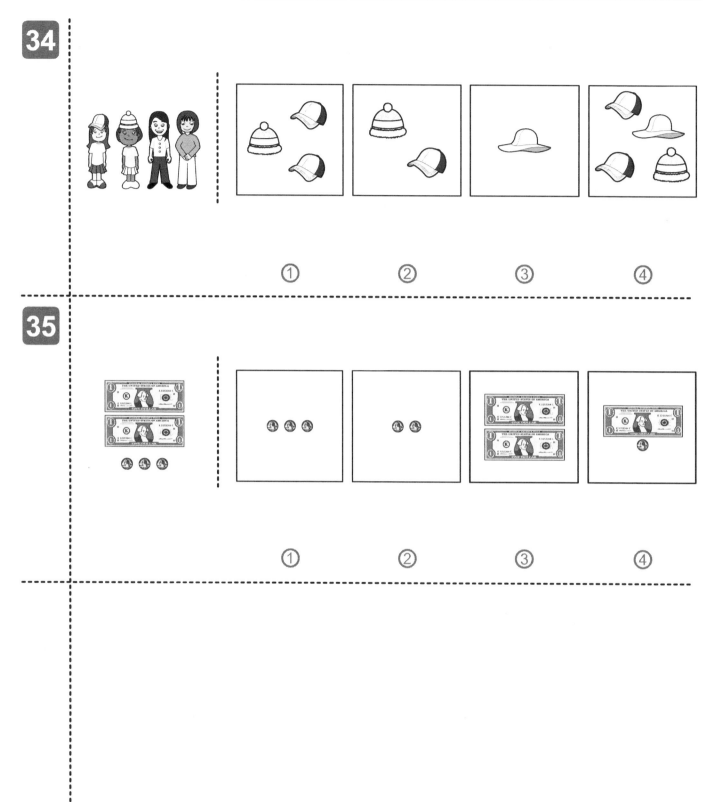

① ② ③ ④

**35**

① ② ③ ④

# Section Four

# Analogies

**OLSAT**® **Preparation Guide II (Level A)**

**01**

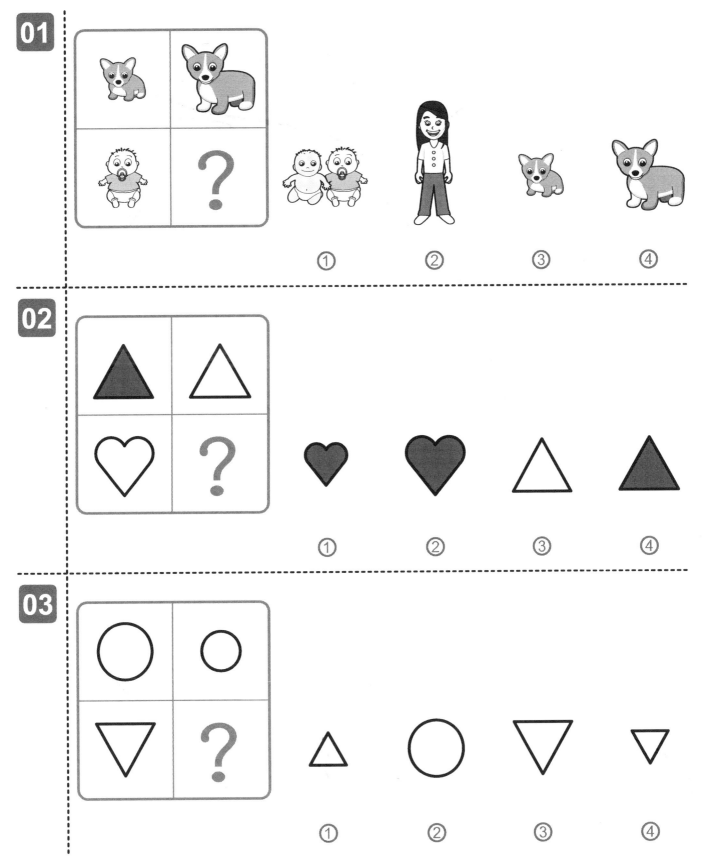

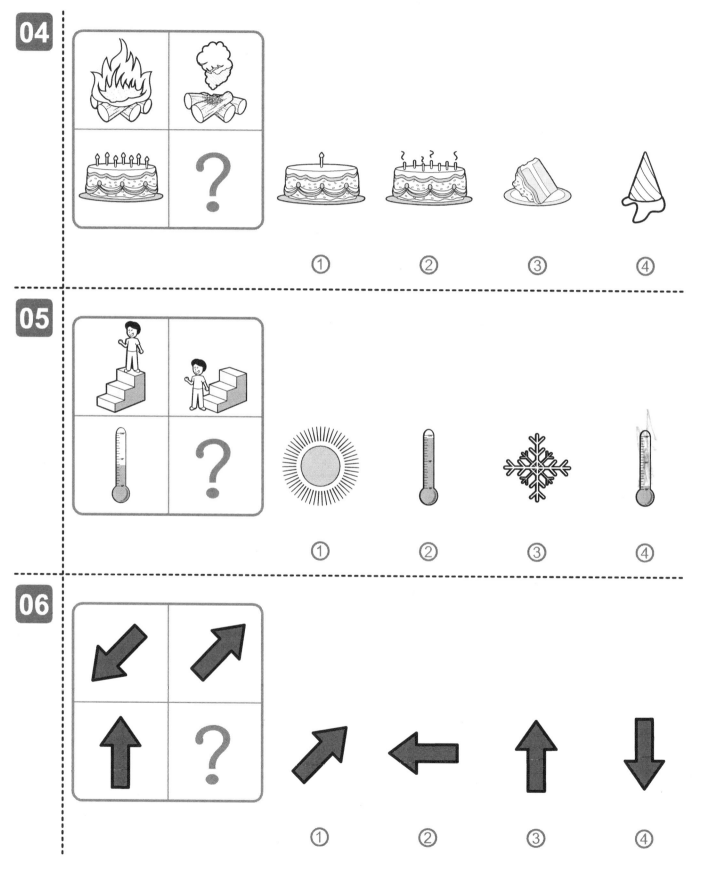

**OLSAT® Preparation Guide II (Level A)**

Bright Kids NYC Inc ©

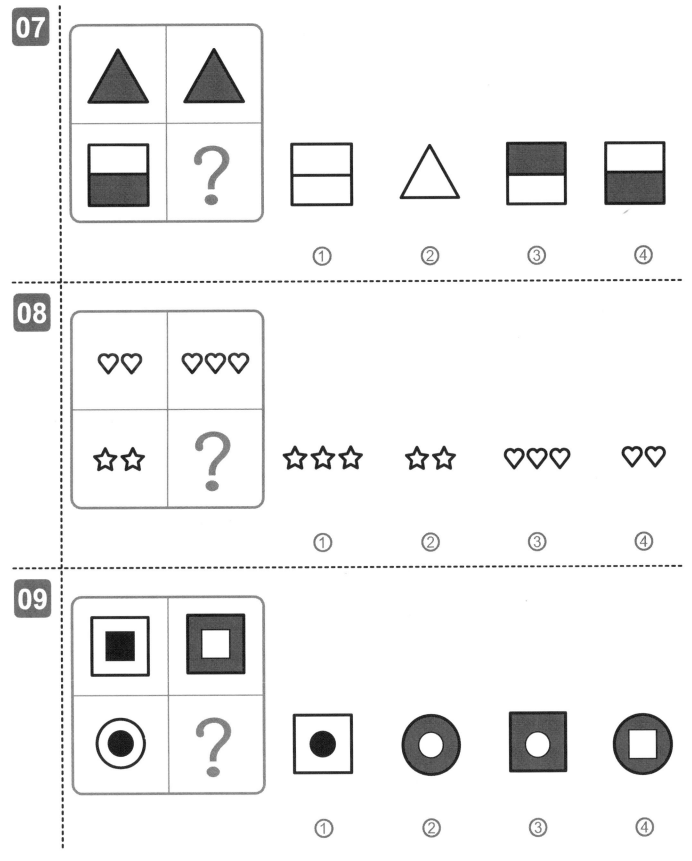

07

08

09

**10**

**OLSAT® Preparation Guide II (Level A)** Bright Kids NYC Inc ©

**13**

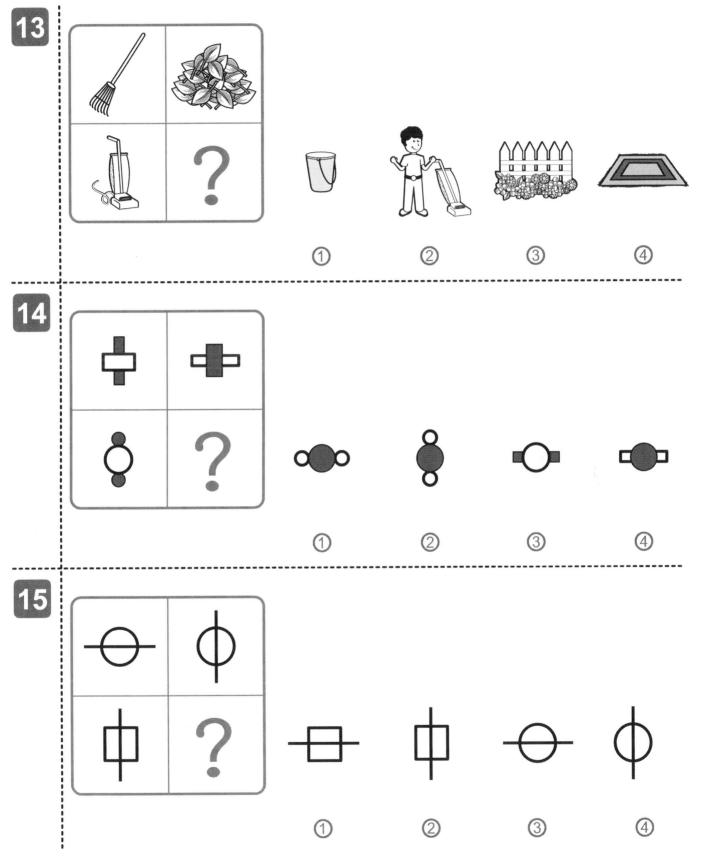

**16**

**17**

**18**

**19**

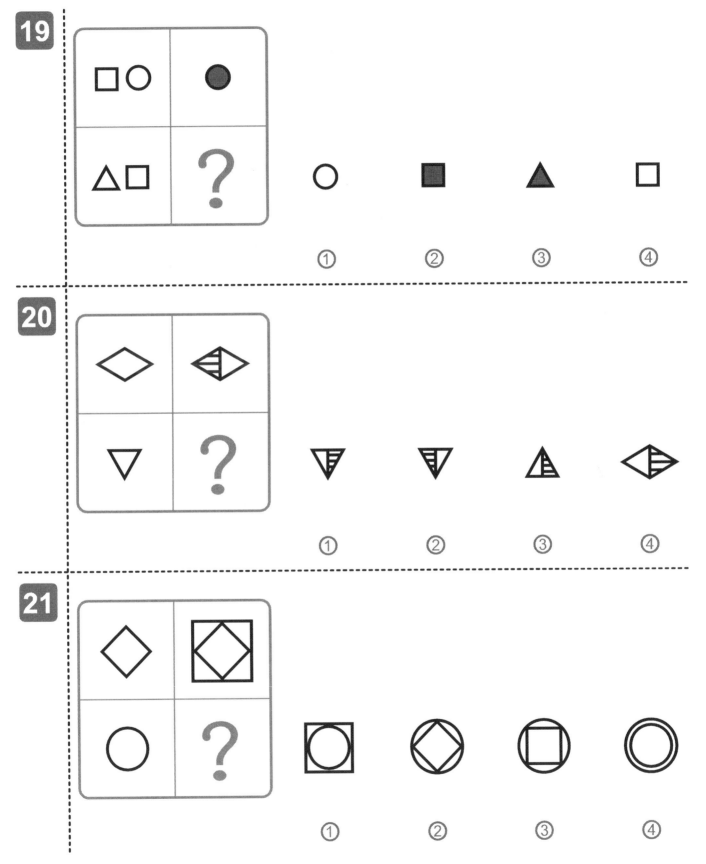

**22**

**23**

**24**

**25**

**26**

**27**

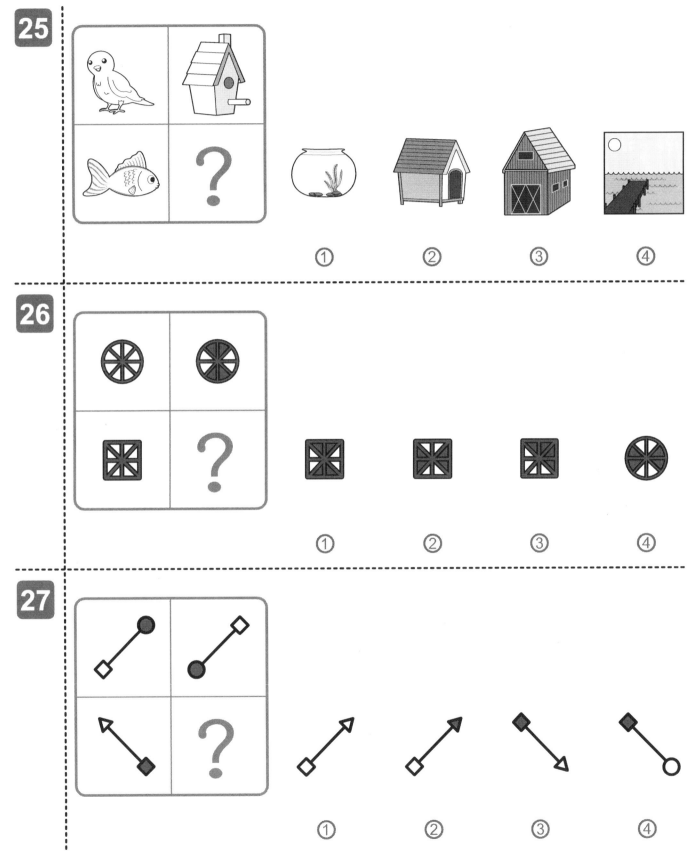

**28**

①  ②  ③  ④

**29**

①  ②  ③  ④

**30**

①  ②  ③  ④

**31**

**34**

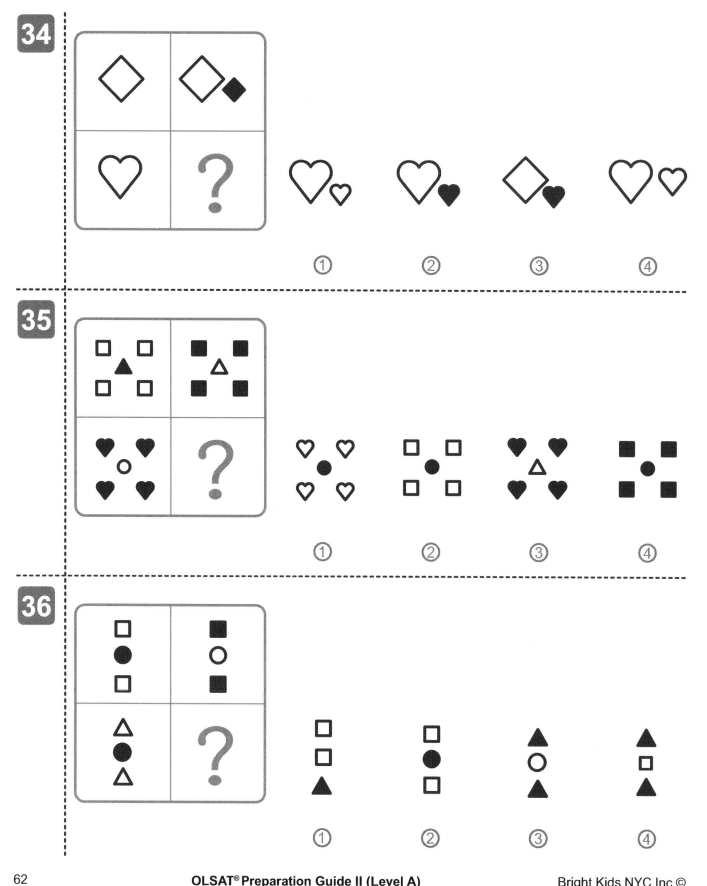

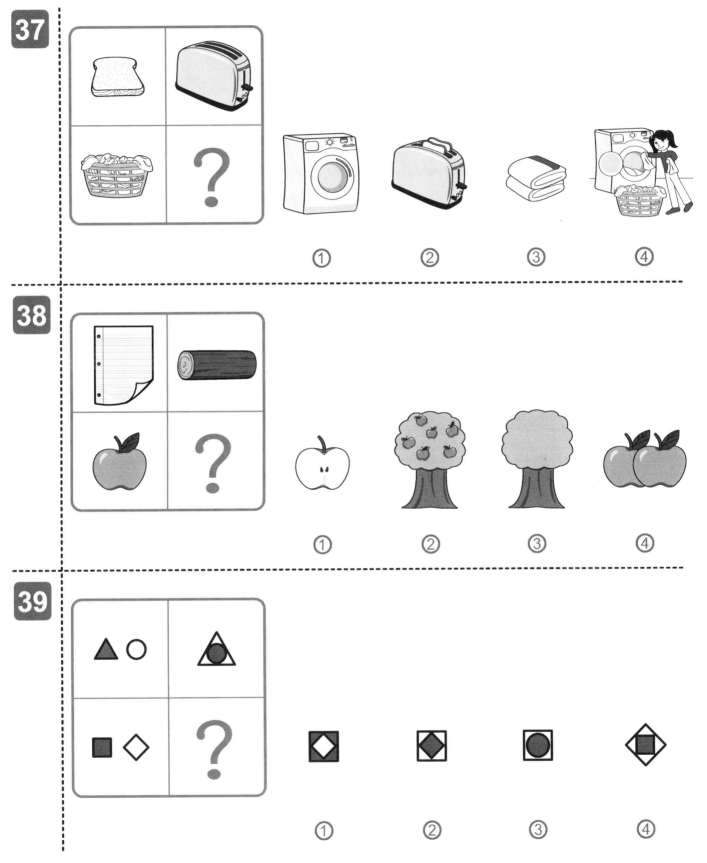

**37**

**38**

**39**

① ② ③ ④

**40**

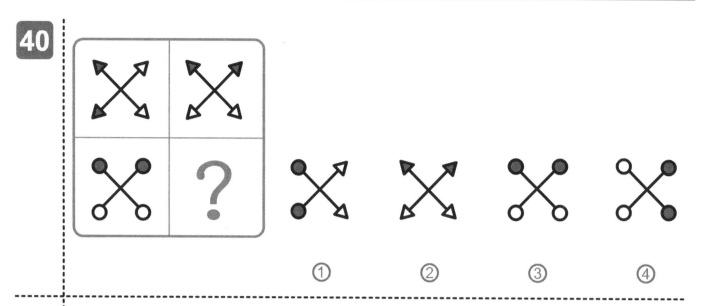

①      ②      ③      ④

# Section Five

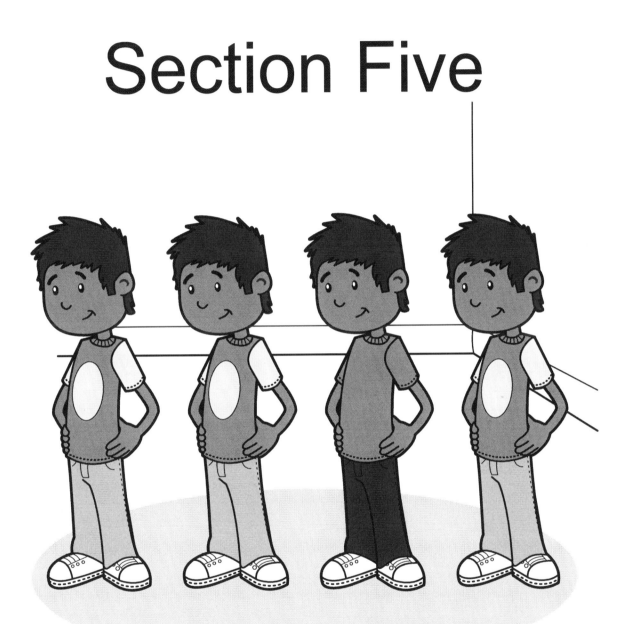

# Classifications

**OLSAT® Preparation Guide II (Level A)**

**01**

①      ②      ③      ④      ⑤

**02**

①      ②      ③      ④      ⑤

**03**

①      ②      ③      ④      ⑤

**04**

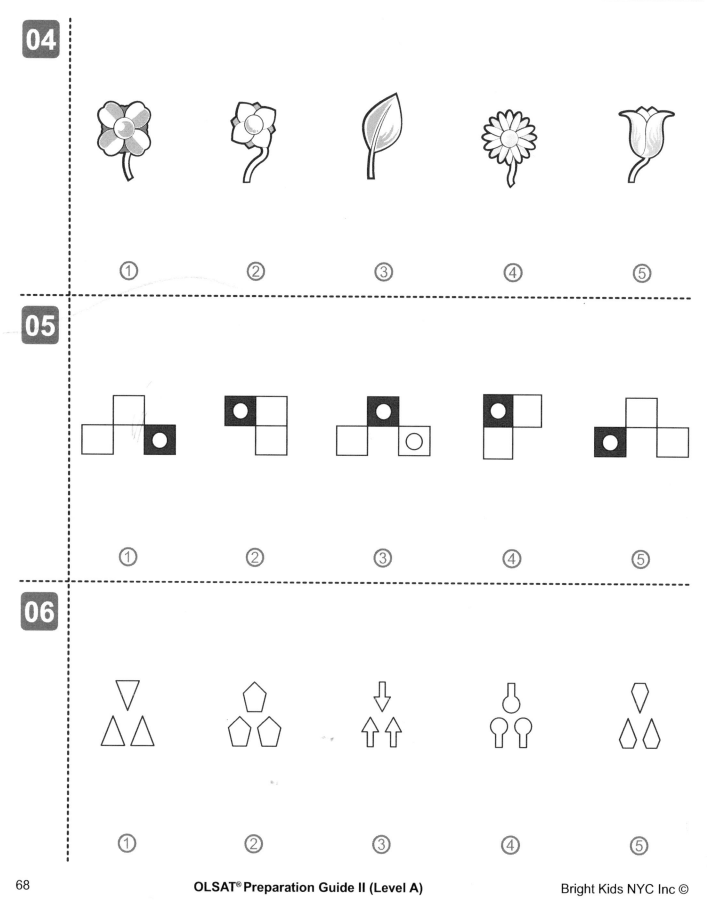

① ② ③ ④ ⑤

**05**

① ② ③ ④ ⑤

**06**

① ② ③ ④ ⑤

**OLSAT® Preparation Guide II (Level A)**

**07**

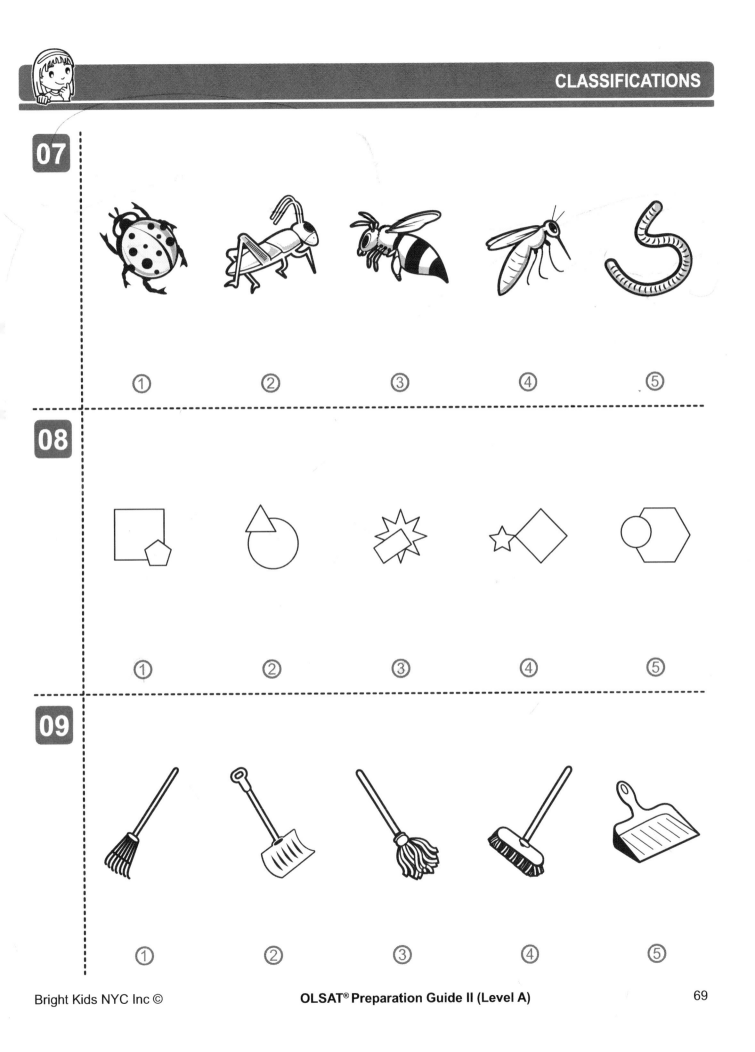

① ② ③ ④ ⑤

**08**

① ② ③ ④ ⑤

**09**

① ② ③ ④ ⑤

**10**

①     ②     ③     ④     ⑤

**11**

①     ②     ③     ④     ⑤

**12**

①     ②     ③     ④     ⑤

**13**

①      ②      ③      ④      ⑤

**14**

①      ②      ③      ④      ⑤

**15**

①      ②      ③      ④      ⑤

**16**

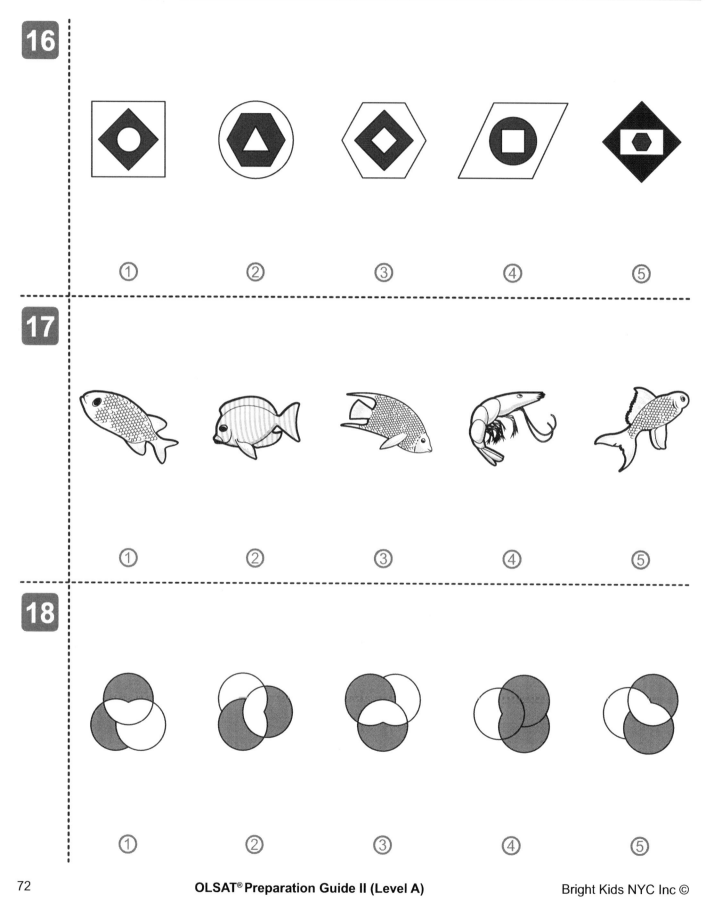

①      ②      ③      ④      ⑤

**17**

①      ②      ③      ④      ⑤

**18**

①      ②      ③      ④      ⑤

**19**

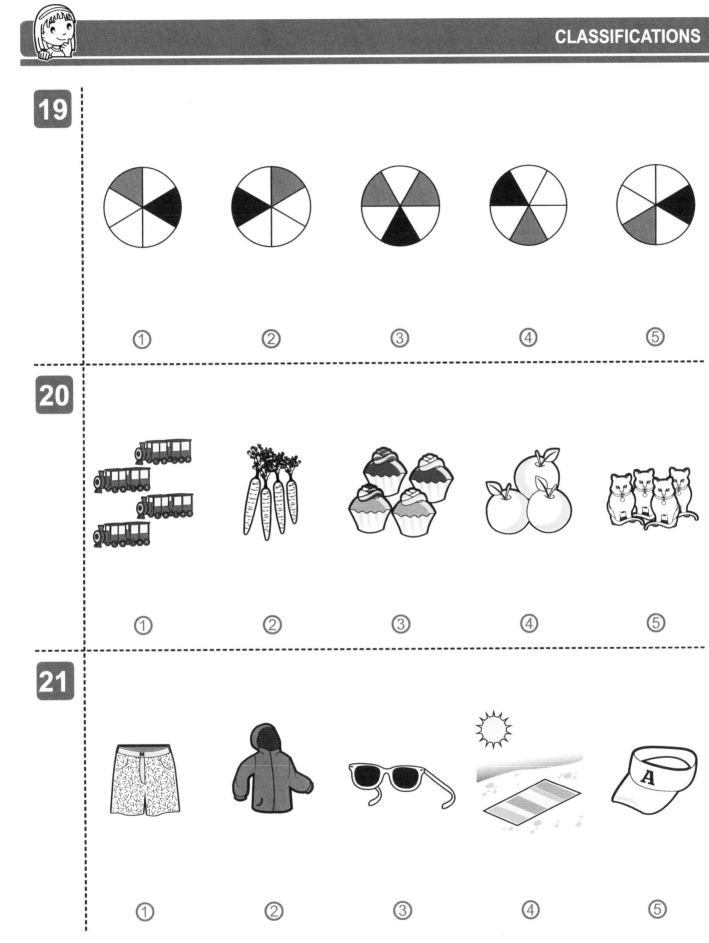

① ② ③ ④ ⑤

**20**

① ② ③ ④ ⑤

**21**

① ② ③ ④ ⑤

**22**

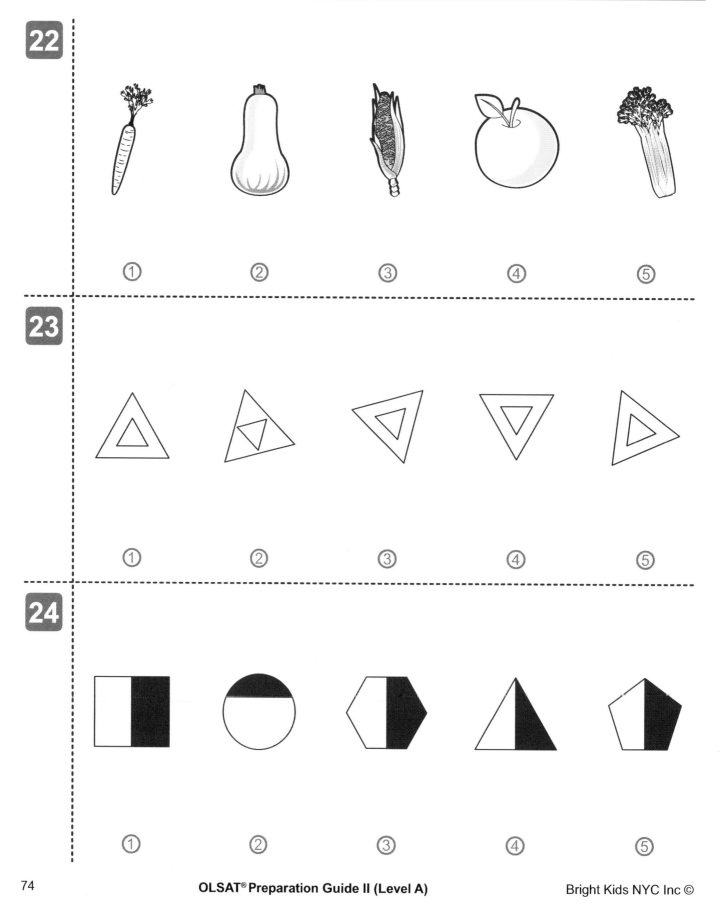

① ② ③ ④ ⑤

**23**

① ② ③ ④ ⑤

**24**

① ② ③ ④ ⑤

**25**

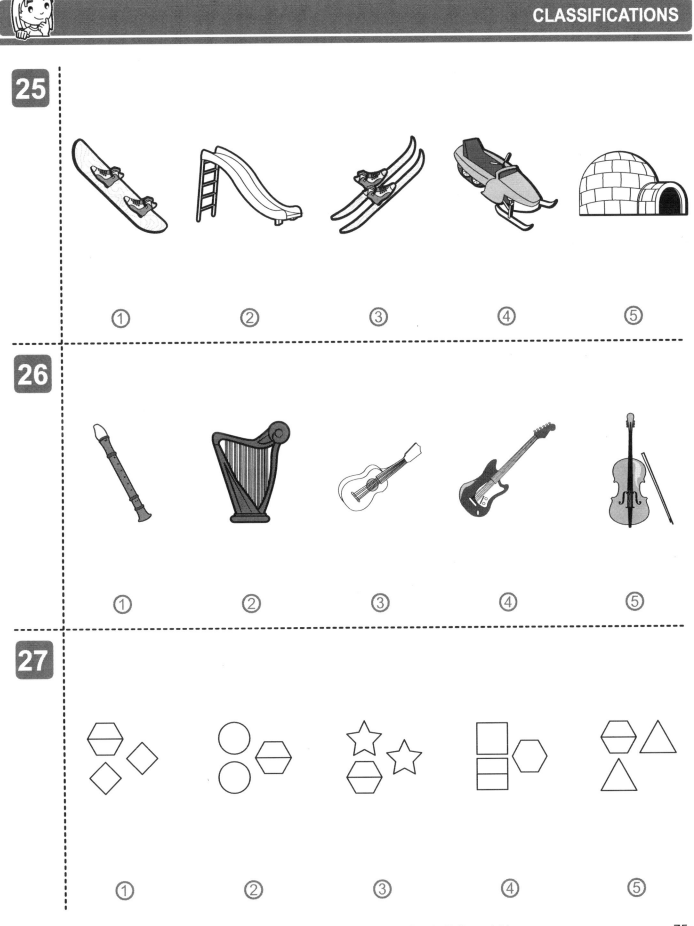

①      ②      ③      ④      ⑤

**26**

①      ②      ③      ④      ⑤

**27**

①      ②      ③      ④      ⑤

**28**

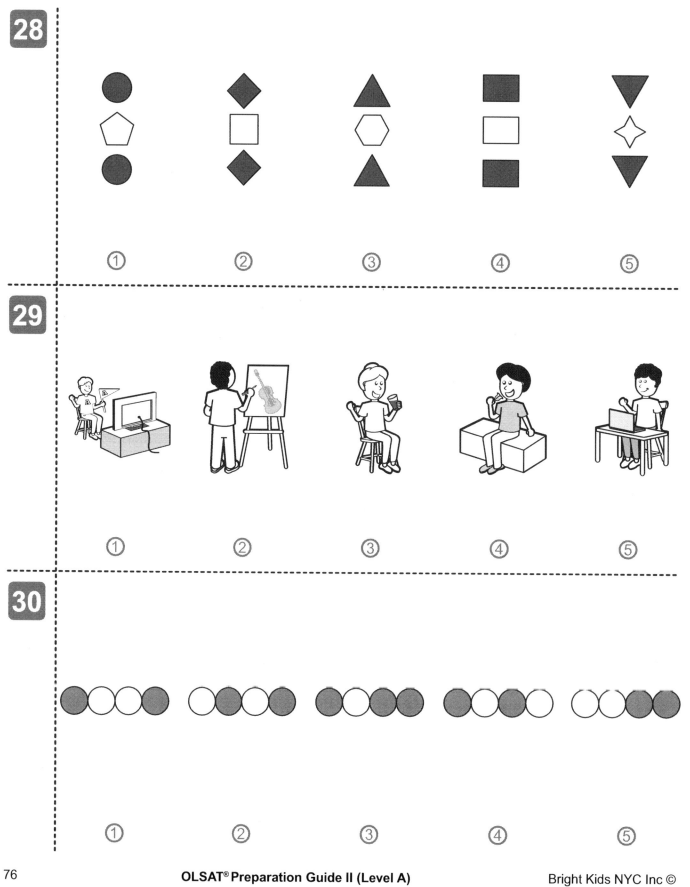

① ② ③ ④ ⑤

**29**

① ② ③ ④ ⑤

**30**

① ② ③ ④ ⑤

**31**

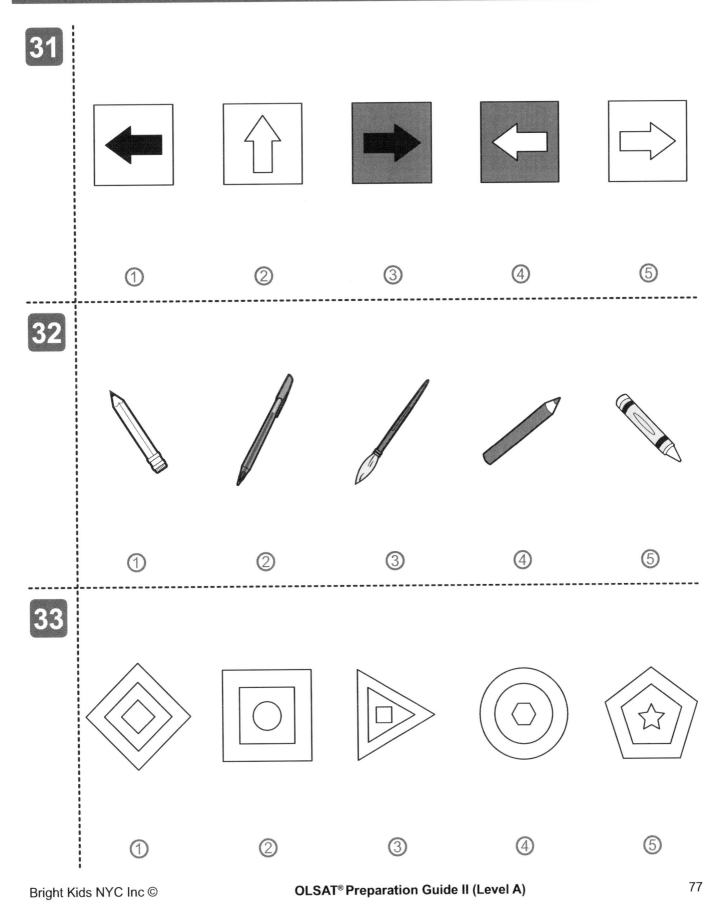

①     ②     ③     ④     ⑤

**32**

①     ②     ③     ④     ⑤

**33**

①     ②     ③     ④     ⑤

**34**

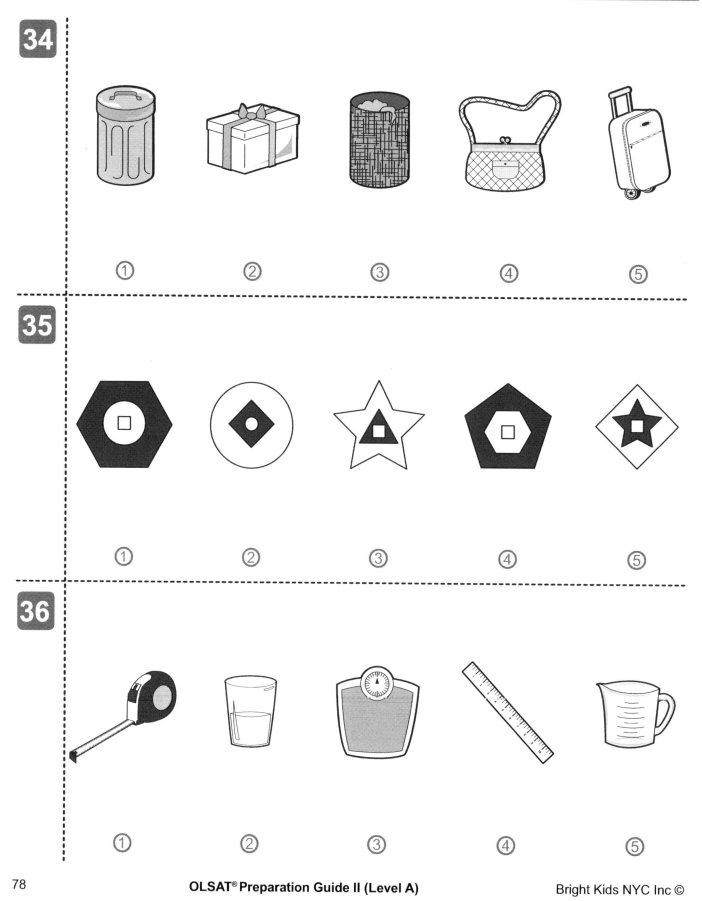

① ② ③ ④ ⑤

**35**

① ② ③ ④ ⑤

**36**

① ② ③ ④ ⑤

**OLSAT® Preparation Guide II (Level A)** Bright Kids NYC Inc ©

**37**

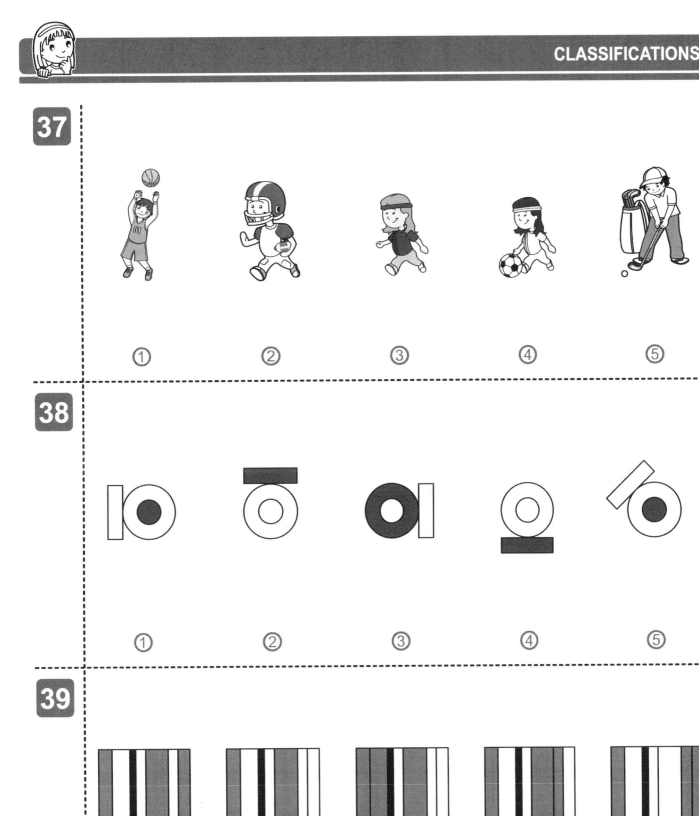

① ② ③ ④ ⑤

**38**

① ② ③ ④ ⑤

**39**

① ② ③ ④ ⑤

**40**

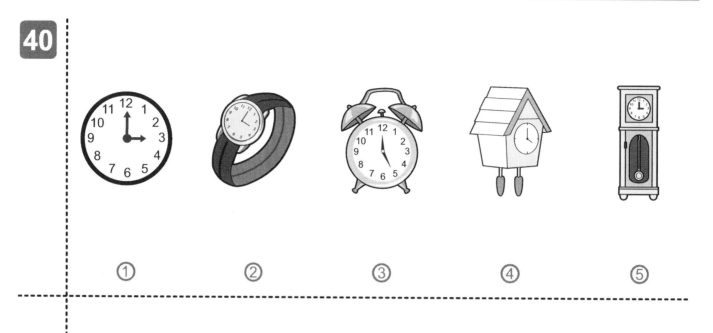

①       ②       ③       ④       ⑤

# Section Six

# Series and Pattern Matrices

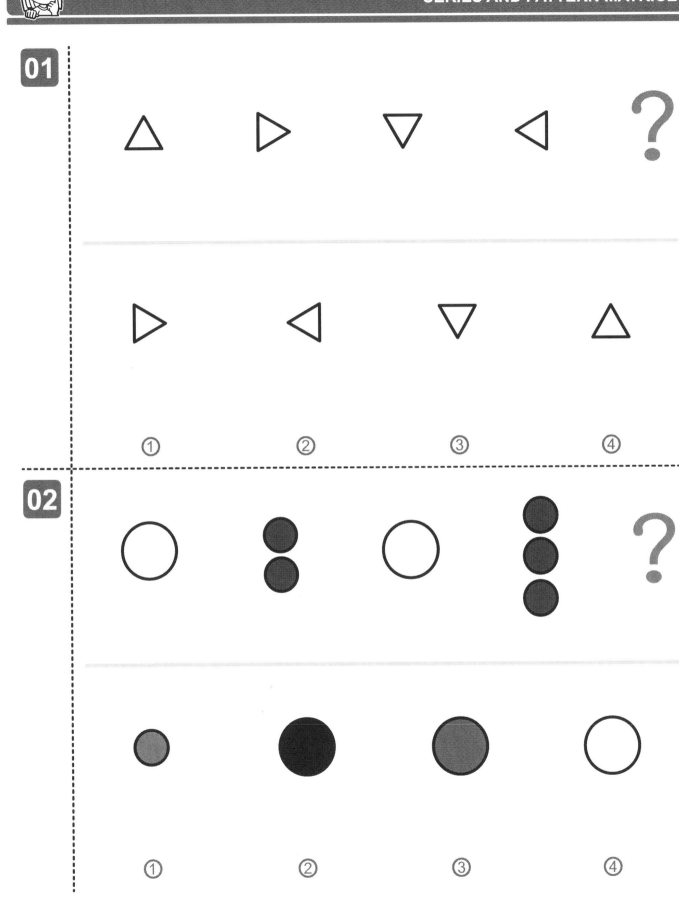

**03**

**04**

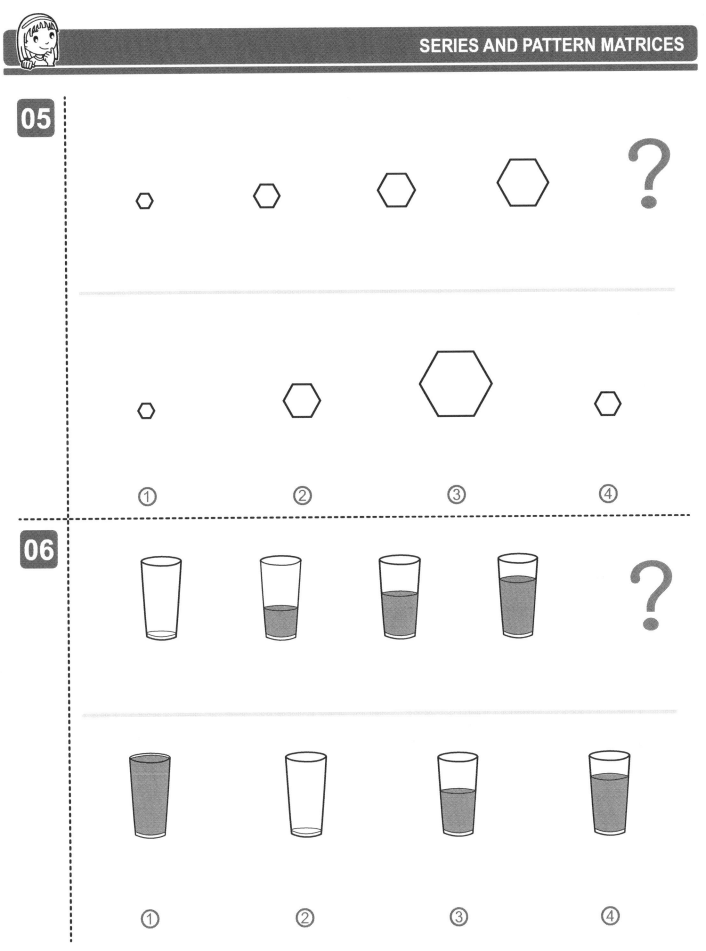

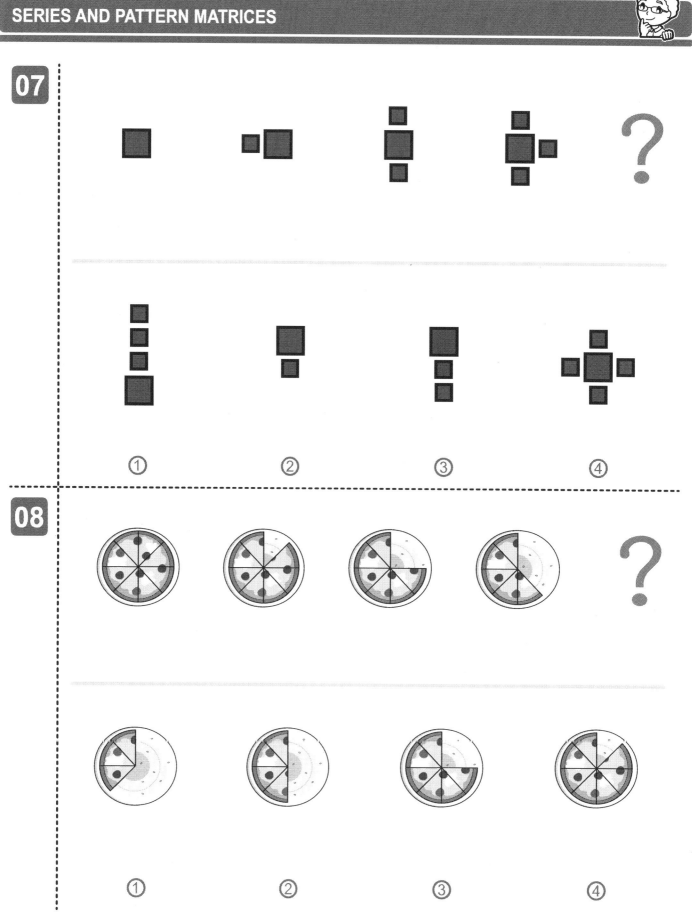

**OLSAT® Preparation Guide II (Level A)** Bright Kids NYC Inc ©

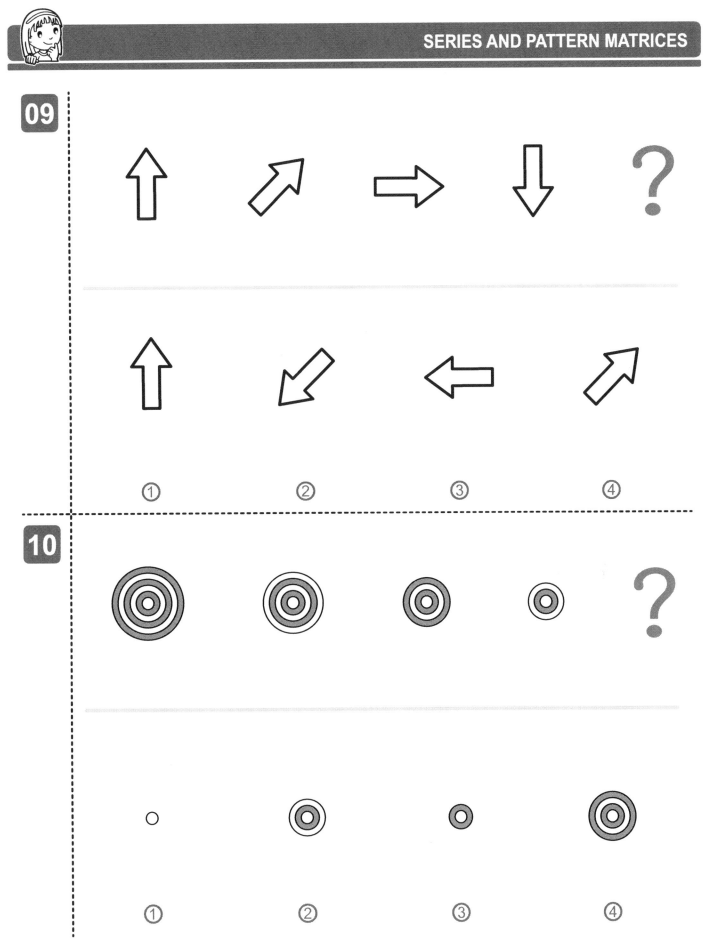

**09**

**10**

**11**

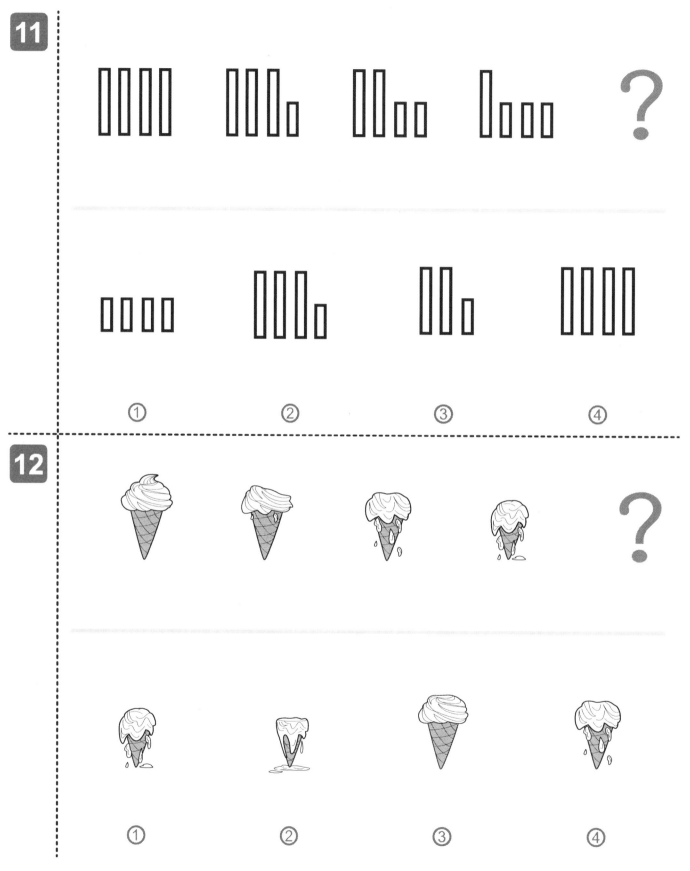

① ② ③ ④

**12**

① ② ③ ④

**13**

① ② ③ ④

**14**

① ② ③ ④

**15**

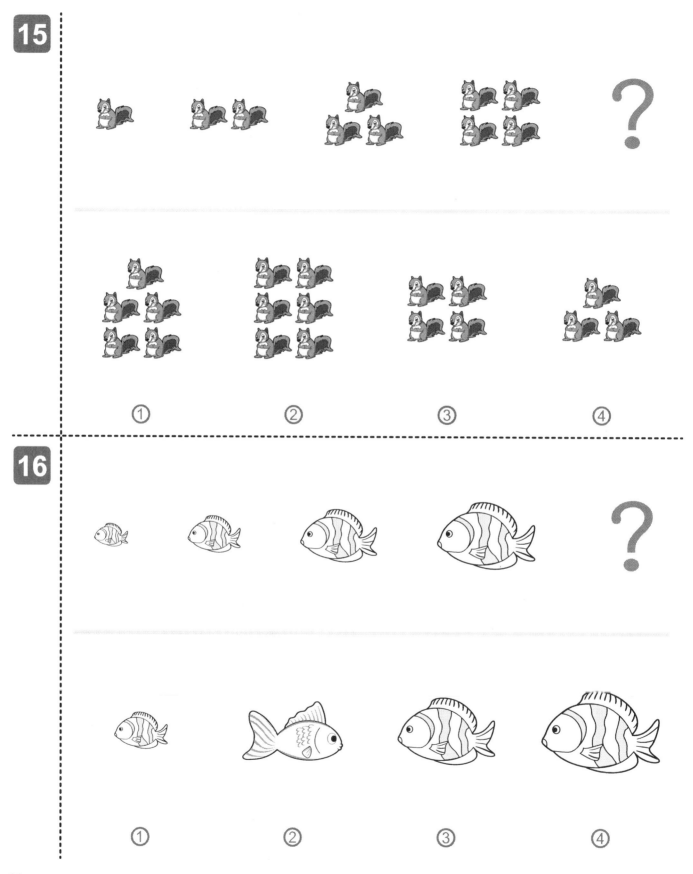

① ② ③ ④

**16**

① ② ③ ④

**OLSAT® Preparation Guide II (Level A)**
Bright Kids NYC Inc ©

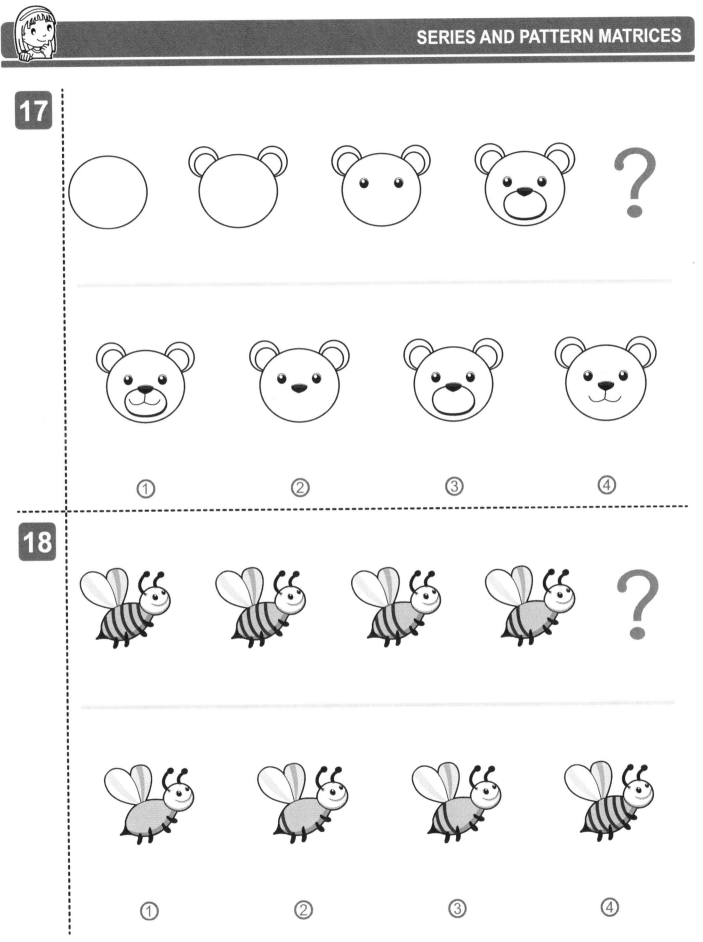

17

①　②　③　④

18

①　②　③　④

**19**

**20**

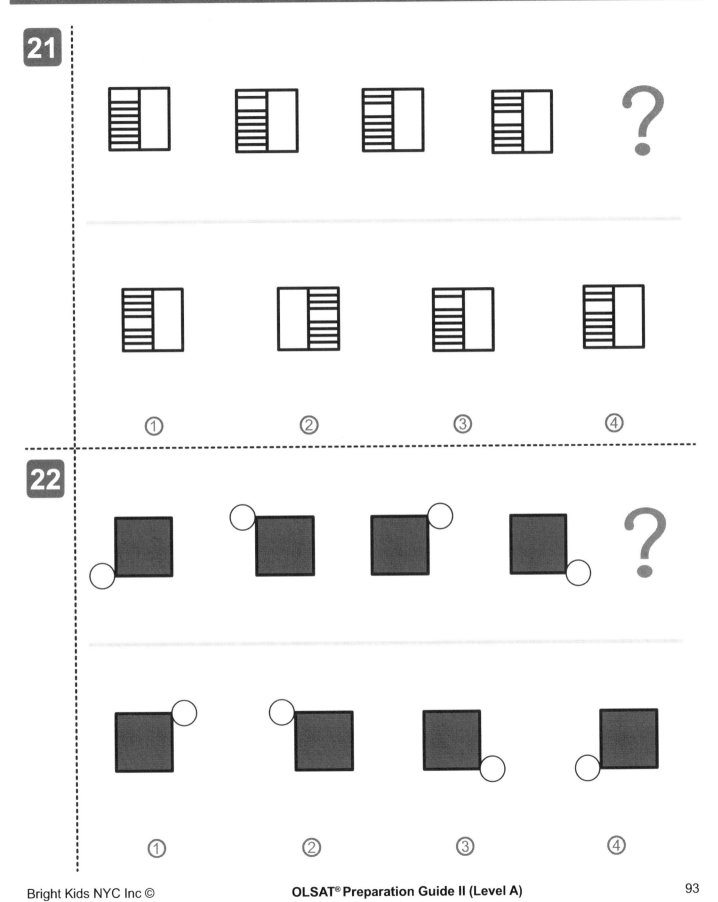

**23**

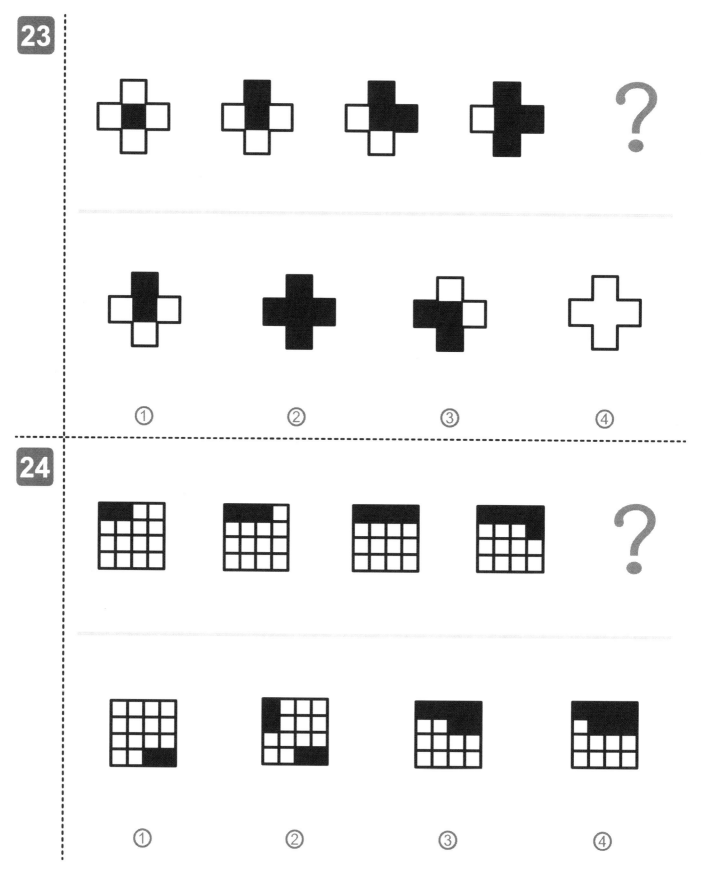

**OLSAT® Preparation Guide II (Level A)**

Bright Kids NYC Inc ©

**25**

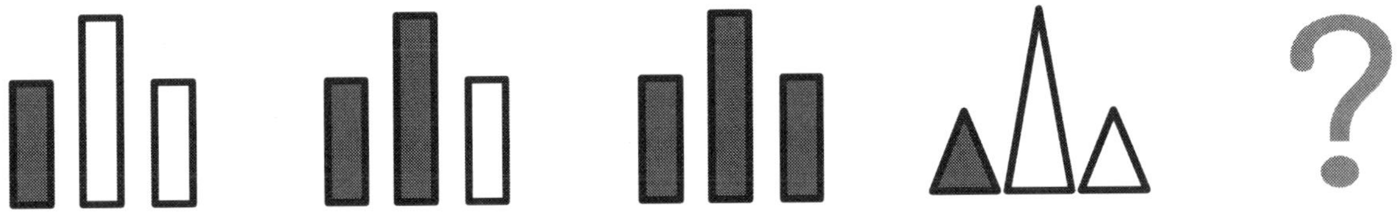

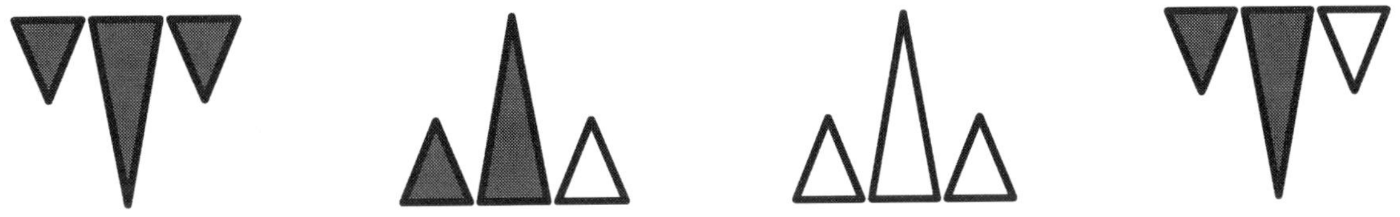

① ② ③ ④

**26**

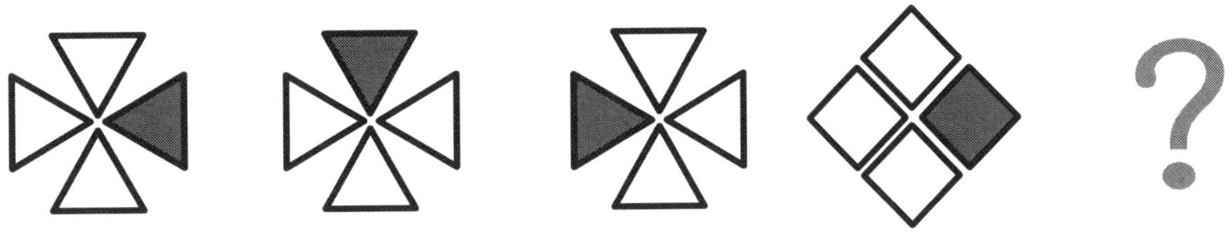

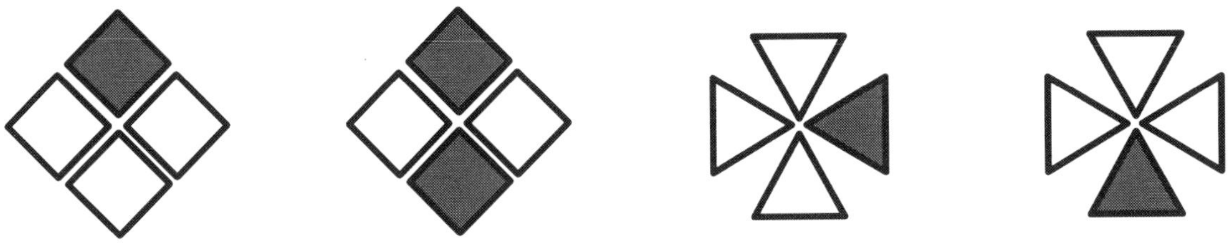

① ② ③ ④

**27**

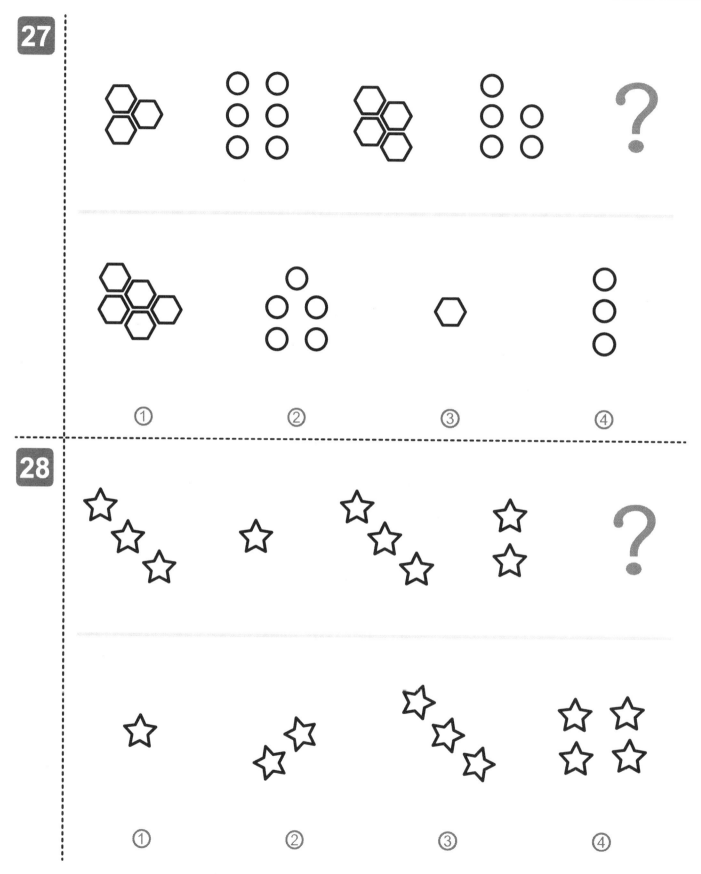

①　②　③　④

**28**

①　②　③　④

**29**

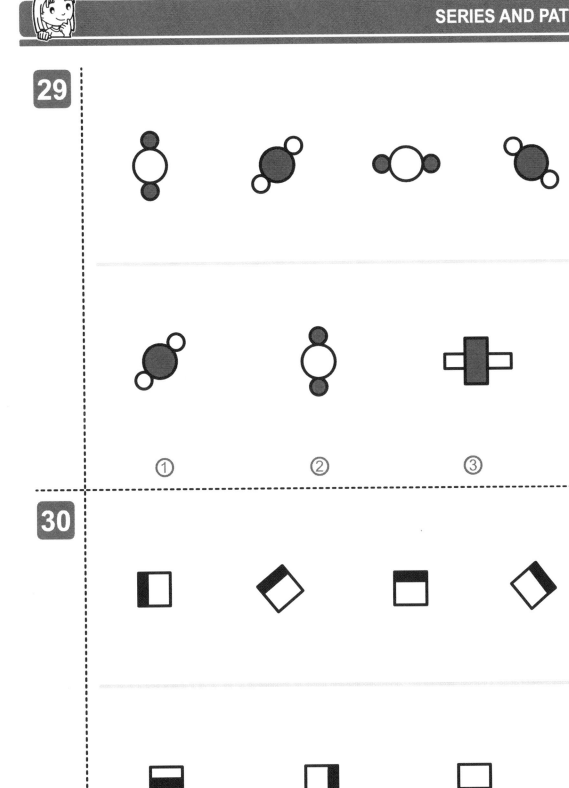

① ② ③ ④

**30**

① ② ③ ④

**31**

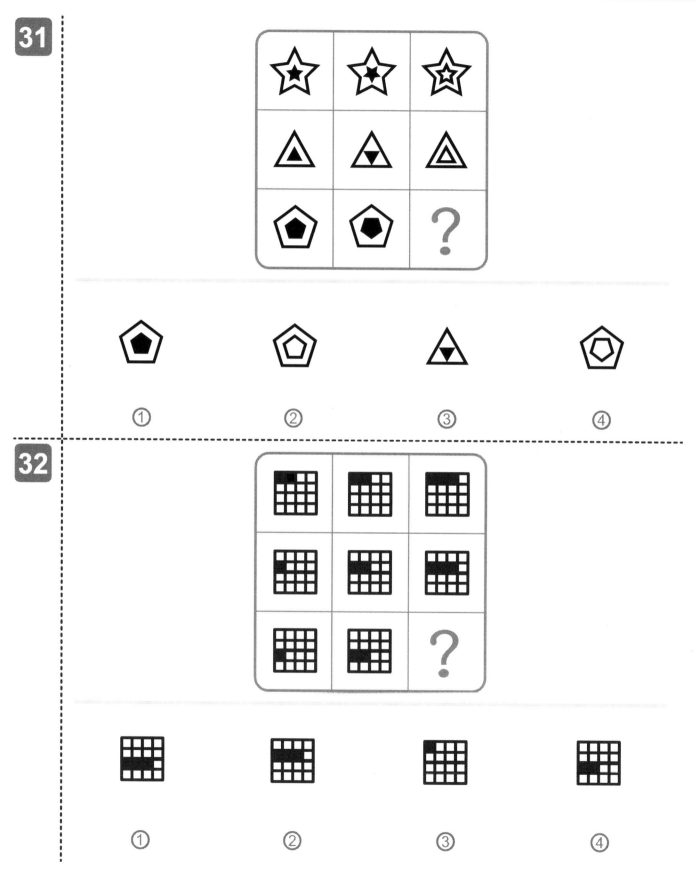

**33**

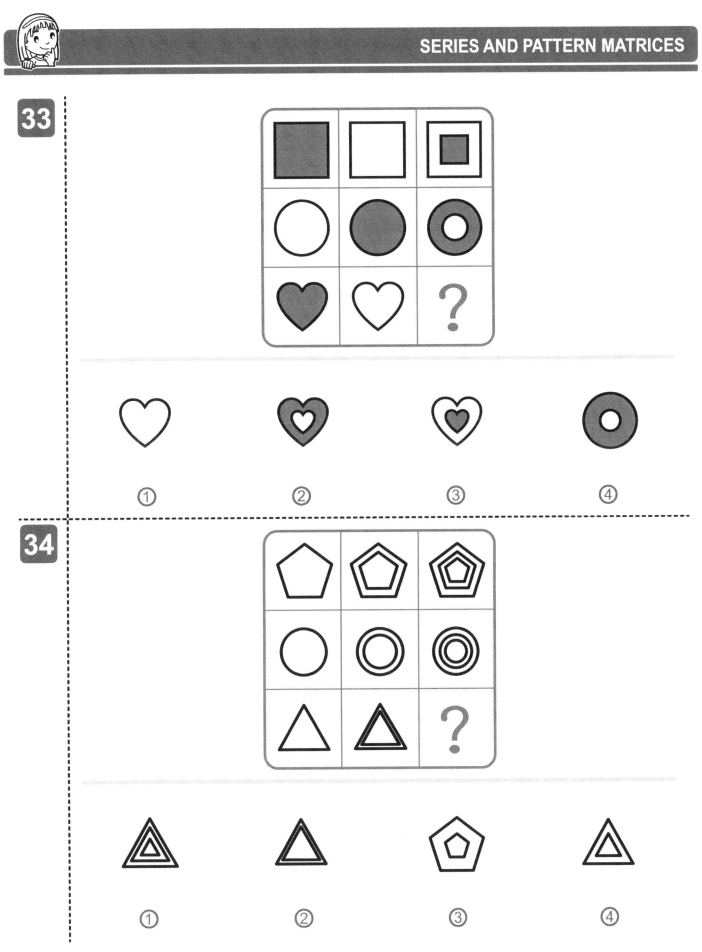

**34**

**35**

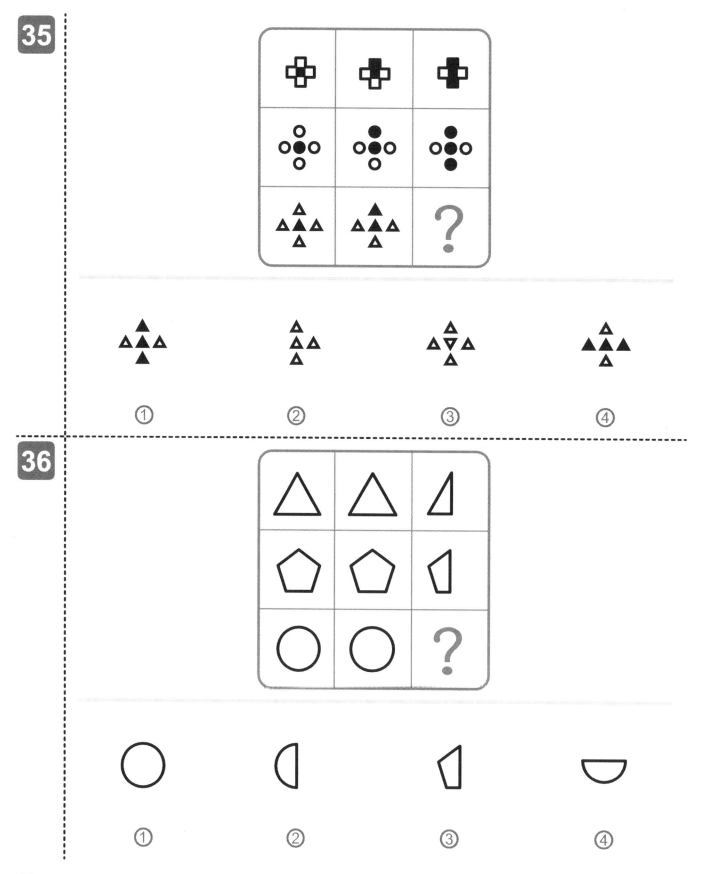

① ② ③ ④

**36**

① ② ③ ④

**37**

| N | Nn | n |
|---|----|----|
| l | li | i |
| M | Mm | ? |

n          m          M          k

①          ②          ③          ④

**38**

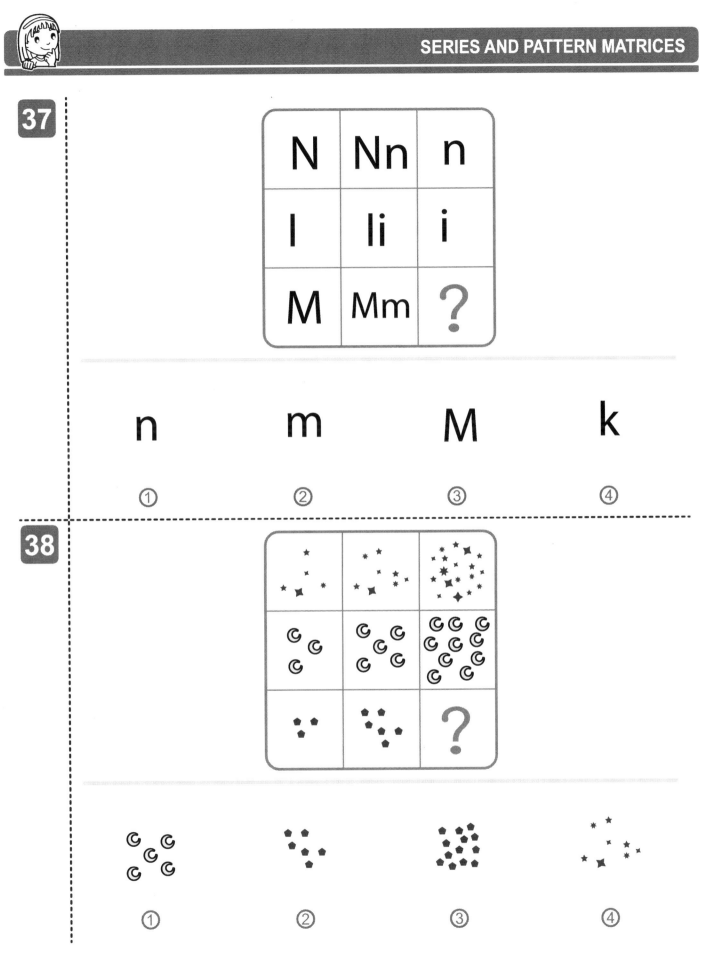

①          ②          ③          ④

**39**

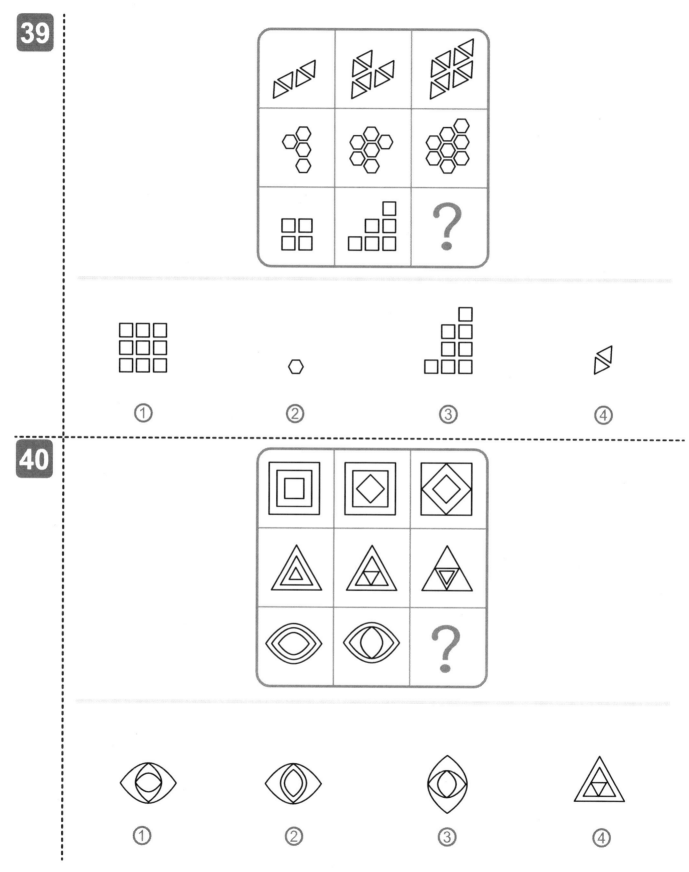

**OLSAT® Preparation Guide II (Level A)**